Praise for **Who Am I? Where Am I?**

"*Who Am I? Where Am I?* is a fascinating read. Unlike any other book that I have ever read, this book is designed for self-discovery of the physical and non-physical world. If you are looking for guidance on how to experience greater sense of peace of mind, look no further."

Peggy McColl
New York Times bestselling author

"Mouna Saquaque endeavours and succeeds in answering and explaining some of life's toughest questions in *Who Am I? Where Am I?* A thoughtfully written and well-crafted take on the questions that many have spent their lives trying to answer. Saquaque manages to offer answers to every reader who has ever pondered these thoughts throughout their lives."

Maria Steuer
International bestselling author of *Breaking Your Loyalty Contract*

"Mouna Saquaque has written a must-read book for anyone considering to know oneself better. It is the dissection of "I" in its full glory. The book is thought provoking and makes the reader travel through the various aspects of "I" (one's own self) and finally arrives at the most astonishing conclusion. The highest philosophy presented in a simpler way for one to relate to and understand."

Sandeep M Agarwal
Author of *Working through the Infinite Source*

"Mouna Saquaque takes you on a fascinating journey of self-awareness. She travels down a road that causes you to think very deeply about your beginning and everything between to the end. The content of this book will inspire you to seek answers within yourself. I highly recommend this book to all that desire a higher awareness and want to know *Who Am I? Where Am I?*"

Tony Douglas
International bestselling author of *Discerning the Voice of God by the Leading of The Holy Spirit*

WHO AM I? WHERE AM I?

From a Human Perspective

MOUNA SAQUAQUE

Published by
Hasmark Publishing International
www.hasmarkpublishing.com

Permission should be addressed in writing to Mouna Saquaque at mounasaquaque.com

Editor: Gary Hoffman
gary@hasmarkpublishing.com

Cover & Layout: Anne Karklins, Kelly Kinsman
anne@hasmarkpublishing.com

ISBN 13: 978-1-989756-25-6
ISBN 10: 1989756255

DEDICATION

A poem for Mom

How do you do, Ô divine Mother?
Love Incarnation of the Higher
Thank you for accepting this role, Pro,
That you played with Maestro.

So many times, I try to give
From the beginning, I only receive
Never being able to conceive.

In the game of child and Mother
Newborn in advance surrender
Confused, little cannot gather
How someone cherish him so tender.

For only a fool thinks he might
Render to the sun, its luminous bright
By starting a fire with a candle light.

Your acts transcend all logic
Try to defy laws of physics
Took me a while to let you space
'Cause you taught me at my pace.

Most never seem to realize
Unless a day they become wise
Enough to see and recognize
That Mom is a gift from paradise.

Blessed forever, now is not late
For carrying who will populate
Earth's Kingdom governorate.

When a Mother becomes a Mom
She gets wings, it's not random
Sent from Celestial to bottom.

With Love and Appreciation

Contents

CHAPTER 1

THE PHYSICAL MATTER DIMENSION

1.

"I" GETS PHYSICAL

I leave my mother's womb, and go out into what we might call the Human realm.

My first reaction is to cry. It may be due to the double shock of being separated from all I have known up until this point, together with going from immersion in liquid to immersion in air. It is a radical change, albeit a natural one.

Or, perhaps I cry from relief and excitement? Relief at discovering that what has been waiting for me outside can be navigated, and excitement at realizing that new experiences await? My adventure as an individual now begins in this new space-time reality.

"So" many changes! I no longer have direct access to food; I no longer have my sustenance provided automatically. When hunger manifests, I must somehow signal my need. Until I become confident that my needs will be met, I simply repeat my first reaction; I cry. I cry to be fed. Despite still being strongly attached to my mother, my world has dramatically changed.

I realize that I now have a body of my own by unknowingly testing its limits; by biting or scratching in turn my hands, my toes, my face. I also begin to appreciate that there is a world beyond this new body.

As the days pass, I learn to distinguish light, darkness, colors, and shapes; I have the use of my physical eyes for the first time, and I discover sights in the new world.

I sense roughness, and I sense softness. I sense temperature, in the air, on the fabrics, on my mother's skin. My senses sharpen with their use, with the perception of differences. I learn from experience.

My sense of taste is first exercised with my mother's milk. As I am presented with other options, I begin distinguishing between pleasing and less pleasing tastes; between sour and sweet, salty and bitter.

All these things often have a specific odor attached to them, and so my sense of smell is activated too.

Sight, touch, taste, smell, then sound. Meaningless sounds at first, then I discover that sound can form words. By hearing these sounds repeatedly, I begin to understand that they have meaning. They represent something: an object, an idea, a directive, a request, an expression of emotion.

I spend much of my time in this new world on a bed, but from time to time I discover the world while being carried on shoulders, sitting on laps, or cradled in arms. Later, I will be discovering the world by crawling, walking, running. As I explore, I realize that I no longer want to be a decoration. I want to participate, to interact with the outside world that I am beginning to appreciate the vastness of.

I navigate from crib to room, from room to house, from house to street. I see more rooms, more houses, more streets. This world seems infinite.

The infinite world may have infinite dangers, which the people entrusted with my care, the adults, explain to me. I need to be aware of the things I should pay attention to. Their concern is sometimes to protect me, sometimes to keep me close and subject to their watchful eyes; they want to make sure that they do not lose track of me or see me in danger. Many such warnings are valid. Most warnings seem wacky, but are born of a desire to protect what is still a very fragile being. Their sense of being vigilant, is, I discover later, larger than their actual vigilance.

So here I am: at last endowed with an independent physical body and five senses enabling my interaction with the physical world.

The body I have been given is an anatomical vehicle; sort of an avatar.

While some people are quite content with their physical apparatus, others don't like it at all. Very rarely are people completely satisfied in the skin they have been given.

The starting point for this avatar is a result of genetic history, species evolution, the nutrition it receives and the environment in which it evolves. Later, conventions of health, shape, weight, and beauty may influence it as well. It all adds up to a continuous transformation of this body from its birth to its death. As we come to appreciate these factors, it is apparent that this body, this avatar, is a fascinating machine despite its fragile origin and destiny.

This physical body is derived from Earth, and to Earth it will return as part of a cycle or plan. Thus, we know that mankind body is an integral part of the physical universe. And beyond this body, an individual human shares the environment of this planet with other physical bodies. Bodies representing what we know as other humans, what we know as animals, and what we refer to as "lower" forms of life.

Each human body is essentially an interface between the entity's "inside" world (subjective and individual), with everything that is beyond it in the "outside" world. The inside world is constrained by the apparent limits of the anatomical body, and the outside world contains the rest of reality. Together, they represent the whole of physical reality.

My experience with this environment, this outside world, began at my birth; a radically different environment from where I had been developing in the preceding nine months.

In my new reality, I first identify air, then my mother, then the concept of the space we both occupy. My perception progresses to other people, then to colors and shapes, the sky, the sun, the rain, the clouds, plants, trees, and animals. I begin to understand the idea of "other places." There is our house (the place where we live, sleep, eat) and there is outside. Outside contains other places: other houses (where other people live); the street (a means to go even further afield); places with a specific purpose. Markets, parks, schools, hospitals, other buildings whose purpose I have yet to fully understand at the time.

In schools, adults will continue my training. There, it is no longer about satisfying my whims. I am taught in a continuous, assiduous, rigorous way how to speak, how to write, how to count, how to draw. These lessons can be summed up by one concept: transmitting knowledge to me from the experience of other humans.

My lessons advance over the years, through courses which multiply and become more specific. And in all of these ever expanding, ever more detailed lessons, I realize that all are conveyed with an idea, a belief, a value. But I may not immediately perceive that ideas, beliefs, and values are not always objective in this "outside world." Rather, they sometimes come from the "inside worlds" of other beings, other avatars, meaning that some element of these lessons are subjective; they may not contain objective information or an "objective truth." If I am lucky, I may at some point in my growth come to realize how to recognize the difference.

But in the early lessons, in the interactions with others in the outside world, I have not yet caught on to the fact that there is nothing more subjective than being taught by another human being, despite the fact that it is the only known way to learn anything. The more that your teacher is nice to you, the more difficult it is to reject the contents of the lesson. The more your instructor is someone you admire, the easier it is for you to accept ideas, beliefs and values without questioning their absolute truth.

Therefore, if we are not careful and aware of this pattern, we will believe what we believe not because it is true, but because we believe in the character and motives of the person who taught it to us.

The narrative you are reading is merely my experience of a functional body navigating in an external world where both my body and the rest of the world are composed of matter. These physical manifestations of matter are never truly separated in the entity which I know as "me." Together, they form my experience of an objective world – an objective world in which I stop experiencing when I go to sleep.

From my earliest memories, I have been thirsty for discovery and new experiences. I want to know everything (possible).

As my learning progresses, I notice that adults have an answer for almost everything. And when they don't know an answer, frequently I will be told to "focus on what's more important," to apply what I already know in the course of new discovery.

In the course of discovery, through both query and observation, I begin to distinguish the essential difference in this outside world between what is nature and what is evidence of mankind's taming of nature. The coexistence of both is the story of discovery itself.

Nature can be beyond the power and control of mankind. And yet, nature is the background, the canvas with and upon which man has never ceased to draw.

The ground, for a city girl like myself, is almost completely covered in asphalt. The only times I am in contact with the actual soil is in gardens and parks. There is soil in potted plants, but that soil is brought from elsewhere. Digging in soil, I often find earthworms and grubs.

Away from the city, I discovered more evidence of nature. I discover farms and fields, usually groomed and maintained by humans. I discover mountains, which, as I will learn, have been created by the internal movement of the Earth's crust. I discover expanses of sand, often near large bodies of water.

I see plants, many showing evidence of the hands of Man; these are under the supervision of humans either to grow food or to add beauty to Man's sculptured world. Some people replace the plants they cut, because plants play an important role in our survival, I am told. They produce the oxygen needed to sustain human life.

Where there is not asphalt, or mountains, or vegetation, or sand, there is water. In lakes and rivers but also in oceans and seas. When I was small, we took a trip to the ocean every summer. There, where the water is salted, is where I discovered the beaches, the fish, the crabs. On the horizon, I saw boats on the water; some brought back seafood, some simply brought back the memories of the sailors as they enjoyed the sun and solitude of a day on the water.

Beyond the Earth's surface, I see the sky, full of clouds, stars, planets, birds, and other flying things. I see the sun, which illuminates the planet and signals to me that it is time to wake and start the day. I see the moon, less predictable, less constant than the sun, but whose appearance is usually my cue that the day is ending. There are stars, not always visible, and not always in the same positions, but sparkling and mysterious. I see the moon and stars less often as a child since I am usually asleep when they appear, but on those occasions when I can see them, they fascinate me.

I also learn that animals are another element of nature, beyond mankind. The first animals I encounter are pets, and these almost seem human; they have learned to live with and around us, and respond to our instructions, requests, and moods. Then I meet farm animals, which I have refused to eat when I have met them in person. The wild animals I have seen in films and television shows, and seen depicted in books, are only accessible to me in person at zoos, where we must keep our distance.

Flying things are my window into the wild creature world outside of the zoo. The most common are a variety of insects, ants, and butterflies that fascinate me; I observe them and follow them visually until they disappear from my sight.

But my favorite beasts, majestically mysterious, are birds. When I was little, it seemed they were talking to me, singing for me, telling me something. I would go up to the terrace and give them leftover bread and semolina, but I would need to hide to let them eat it; they seemed to be spying on me, reluctant to approach too closely. Returning with a basket full of food, I would ask them to take me for a tour, but when I saw adults laughing at me when I was doing so, I understood it was impossible. I stopped trying to communicate with the birds, but kept bringing them food.

While on the terrace interacting with the birds, I would spend hours looking at the sky. If I had a companion, I would show them the images I saw in the clouds.

I was not permitted to play in the rain, and I did not understand why until the day I defied the rules and became completely, uncomfortably wet. When it rained, I would place buckets on the terrace, let the rain fill them, and dance in the deep water with my plastic boots.

Mankind's achievements parallel these elements of nature, and to accomplish anything man must either overcome or work around nature. An umbrella or a roof works around rain; a vessel overcomes the sky or the ocean. And part of my education consists of learning the difference between what nature provides and what mankind accomplishes.

As a little girl of the city, my belief was that the city is the natural environment for humans. The countryside, in my experience, was for those who volunteered to spend time in a less comfortable place, providing the rest of us with fruits, vegetables, and meat. Beyond the countryside, no one could survive without the talents and wit of a Robinson Crusoe.

Immediately after my birth, "I" get aware of my physical apparatus and the physical universe (earth, skies, and their other physical inhabitants) that surrounds me through the sensory factors that I have at my disposal. However, this is not how it all begun. Let's go deeper into it in the next chapter.

2.

TIME TRAVELLING TO MY PHYSICAL ORIGINS

As a human, I was not a physical witness to the creation of the universe, of the Earth and the heavens. But I have been given some amazing information on that story, how it began, and how I emerged from Earth. I am dust, clay, and water that transformed into this human organism. In my genome, and in the field of this universe, traces and tracks have been left for us. I can retrace some of this story. "I" the body, in a sense, am one with the physical universe. I have arisen from it.

I was initially pure law, an abstraction of an abstraction; then I began to solidify. As I matured and gathered enough energy to have mass, I was released and began to be deployed.

So, once I was not, and then I was; the concept of "self" is itself an object. To my "self," everything existed only on the mental plane (chapter Creation Realm): first an idea, then an intention, then a concept, and finally, matter: a physical manifestation.

Where to actually begin is a delicate question; from nothingness (absolute emptiness, the absence of all objects) to something; passage or evolution from a primordial cause to a thing, which itself is primordial to another thing. Or rather, a passage from nothing (deep sleep) to a world of objects (concepts, energy, matter, space, time).

Origin, therefore, is neither a starting point nor a primary cause. Rather, it can be thought of as the union of conditions allowing the birth of the world of objects, the physical world being the result, and long time after, my physical body.

Given this background knowledge, let us understand the states which my ancestors and I have gone through. This is our story; this is my history as a physical body.

After the mental plane of creation plan (i.e. Creation Plane) was revealed, the deployment started. The physical universe started unfolding, taking a physical form. The Sensible reality (as opposed to the invisible one) begun. So, what does it mean, practically? It means that the physical plane, that is a direct effect of the mental one, begun.

In other words, it was the release, the transformation of energy in space, time, and matter.

These three main components of the physical universe (space, time, and matter) together can be thought of as a cosmic clock, each tick of which transforms the universe from one state to another. Each moment creates a new snapshot of the universe. Combine them, and it is like a photo album of a person showing a progression from child to adult. You can turn the pages of this album until you arrive at the day of your birth, or even now, if you are reading these lines.

Let me take you back in time; let's dare go back in memories.

After this release, after this Big Bang, energy gathered enough mass to become particles. This is the most important time of your life! This is how it got physical, and no entities knew it back then, only later was revealed the plan that you would be sent here in a physical body.

Each particle of matter – including the ones which constitute my physical body – is encoded with laws of physics which must be obeyed. An electron, for instance, knows what to do when it meets another electron.

We know this must be true because if a single interaction had not happened in accordance with the laws of physics, the universe and its inhabitants would not exist as they are today. There are never coincidences in nature's results, although nature's parameters may be temporarily hidden from our understanding.

The space twists around me, rather indistinctly. After being a movement that looks like a spark, I go through some smaller states and then become an electron, then an atom. With each interaction, new atoms are formed. Atoms collide. Movements of repulsion and attraction cause collisions, which begin to generate clouds of dust. I don't see much, and it's still dark.

Combinations of these different elements gradually form dust and astral rocks, and for some reason, it disturbs my mind to realize that certain elements combine or bond with others; it may not be a coincidence that as humans we live together on (and with) Earth because we are both made mostly of water.

Let's return to the idea of "me" as dust, comets, and other astral objects. Collisions continue, things spin everywhere. It's a real whirlwind here. Collisions recur, explosions occur, stars form. Everything swirls in a spiral. It seems that the celestial elements have not yet learned the code of the astral road, nor that it was necessary to drive in its line. The stars have not yet taken their proper places in the firmament; harmony has not yet been reached.

The universe is still in its learning phase, like a wild, untamed child. Various physical objects are jostling to take their proper places. Each state in the universe is the direct consequence of the laws applied to the cause that precedes it. The laws result in the creation of stars, as well as large boulders. As the boulders become larger, they become spherical. The laws of the universe seem to dictate that this spherical shape is the best stable form for big physical objects.

So, "I" am everywhere at the same time, matter swirling madly everywhere. As all of these interactions and exchanges of energy happen, at a certain place in the universe large spheres of rock begin spinning around a certain star, and a solar system manifests.

The rock which will form what we will know as Earth spins and boils. After its collision with another astral object, the moon is formed. This moon will remain in Earth's vicinity and will revolve around it as Earth revolves around the sun. The temperature is hellish at first, but eventually cooling will create a crust which will thicken over time.

Time passes as I decide to stay on this planet. The chaos of creation calms a bit, but comets and meteorites continue landing here. But it hasn't been merely accidental; rather, it seems a primitive way of supplying the planet with everything it will need for its growth and development. Apparently, all of what has happened so far has been for Earth's benefit; I'm glad I followed my instinct and stayed here.

Earth continues to receive iron, hydrogen, and many other atoms from elsewhere. As time has passed, it has cooled well. I don't know how long it took, perhaps billions of years. (Keep in mind that at the time of the planet's formation, solar years would constitute a different objective amount of time compared to what we know as a year today.) It is raining comets and meteorites here, and I wonder what this chaos will lead to.

It's been raining for a while now; the entire universe seems to be interested in this little planet Earth. Little by little, the collisions and interactions cause gas to be released, and now I begin to understand the new concept of chemistry. These gases interact, cool, liquefy, and interact again. "I" am everywhere at the same time, but my interest in Earth continues to grow. As I would say in 2021, "This is the place to be."

Rumors circulate; a "soup" is formed. It roils, becomes agitated, it cooks, it cools, it flows everywhere. I'm still on Earth, and throw myself into this soup. It seems more of magic than of science and physics. Isn't magic everything that we have not yet come to understand? It boils, and starts to act on the rock, making it spongy. Oceans of soup are now on Earth. Thanks to the conditions around me (temperature, pressure, gas...) and the laws that apply to them, something unique happens in the universe.

My concentration, and that of seemingly everything that exists, focuses here. I am living something unique in the cosmos! I bathe in this magical soup until the time that an entity, beyond – but still of – physics and chemistry, is born: a single-celled being. Biology is added to physics and chemistry.

For those of us living in the 21st century as humans, retrograding to being a single-celled life form is as foreign as the idea of charcoal would seem to the brightest diamond. It does not matter; I want to honor all of my physical ancestors, and this journey to the past will tell me a lot about who I really am, at least physically.

Elsewhere in the universe, things continue to happen; reality continues its deployment and evolution. But my attention is held here and now, on Earth, where a unique and unprecedented thing is happening: the birth of life.

Things are developing, although I am not doing anything myself. I am merely an observer. The conditions are right, the necessary elements are in place, the laws of physics are applied, and I observe what is happening in astonishment. What else can I do? I, physically, am merely the result of consecutive causes. I watch the laws of nature being observed. I am the stage and I am the audience. In the form of this cell, I prosper and grow. I develop and multiply, generating forms of life which yearn for exploration.

Some stay in the water, others go on land, and still others develop wings to reach for the sky. Marine, terrestrial, amphibian, or airborne, I want to go everywhere, discover different environments. Movement seems encoded in my genome. This force that moves "me" that's beyond me.

Outside, it now seems less chaotic than the movement of the stars before they learned how to dance. But life still does not seem completely established to me, though at the moment all options seem possible.

As the universe continues on the course of its deployment, all seems calm to me. It is no longer messy or blurry. The atmosphere, created for life, makes the sky beautiful. The sky allows me to access other corners of the universe with my physical eyes. Matter solidifies where there is life. I am mainly here on Earth, in a beast body. I can see stars, constellations, the sun, the moon, the other planets.

I am everywhere at once, but while the universe is one whole body, my attention is mainly focused here on Earth. In this beginning, everything that could grow, flourish, or blossom did so. Trees could grow far taller than the relative shrubs we see today. This is not nostalgia for all which has gone before; if I could bring you a photo from this time, you would be overwhelmed by the diversity and density of life.

In addition to the majestic trees, there are ferocious beasts of such large size and capacity that even the most committed of animal rights activists might shudder. Lions and crocodiles would seem like cuddly toys next to such creatures. In today's vernacular, one might say, "It's a jungle out there!" The rule of "survival of the fittest" takes on a whole new tenor. In the long run, had such monsters survived, everything would have been thrown out of balance. Perhaps that's why meteorological and geological events turned things upside down.

I am not one of those ferocious creatures. Not very tall, and a slightly more agile animal than most, I was omnivorous from the start. I would likely not have survived otherwise. Cataclysms and climate change made Earth a hostile place, so I went into hiding until things settled down. My survival instinct was impressive! It seemed superior to all other animals.

And yet, I'm having a bad time on Earth.

"I" continue to exist with everything, in everything, everywhere, and everywhen. But my attention remains focused on Earth, in this animal that I have dubbed "humanoid."

One day, I come out of my burrow, my cave, to the outside world. Earth, more beautiful and safer than ever, is offered to me. I'm comfortable; I no longer need to hide all the time. I learn to stand up, and my survival skills are sharpened. I'm ready. The humanoid is finally ready to become a human. And this is how my story of experiencing a physical body in a physical world began.

3.

GETTING FAMILIAR WITH LIFE ON EARTH

Very few creatures on Earth survived the great disasters and cataclysms. Among the survivors were several species of humanoids, or hominids. Many animal species looked similar, and it was not uncommon for primates to mate, or live in groups, with hominids. We were omnivores, we shared agility, we foraged for all kinds of berries, we learned to fish and hunt.

But one species of hominids developed more quickly, and more radically. First, this species started to stand on two legs rather than four as a matter of course. While other species might occasionally stand erect during certain activities such as climbing or fighting, this hominid would remain on its hind legs even when not necessary (to the consternation of other species). Walking on two legs made for more agility and meant less fatigue; soon this species became bipedal for good. The art of walking became a reality.

Going beyond our comfort zone, evolving beyond the standards of our original body, being omnivorous all resulted in radical physical changes: on our brain and on our skull; on our skeletal frame and spine; on the alignment of our jaw. Physical transformation began to completely differentiate us from the other hominid species. Some disappeared into extinction, others feared our evolution and newfound abilities and were aggressive towards us.

Perhaps, even more significant than skeletal changes and brain evolution was a change in the larynx, resulting in the ability to emit sounds more clearly and vocalize in a meaningful way. Was it due to the continuous standing position? Was it the developing desire of the brain to inform or warn others? Or was it simply the natural sequence of events to develop the power of speech, and thus the capacity of language and thinking and therefore being ready to receive the Adam mental body (i.e. chapter on Adam).

When those upgrades in our evolution were finished, we were ready for the biggest change that the mental and physical world were preparing for the first time in the history of the universes. A physical (earthly made) entity, man, would possess a separate "mental body." The other mental entities (i.e. chapter on Mental Creation) were skeptical. Some asked, how would this fragile and yet savage being, subject to "unbeing" or death, that arose from earth have the privilege to exist in both a physical and a mental plane? Other entities in the universe were relieved that they did not have to carry such a burden.

And this is the biggest event in humanity, where we becoming sapiens. And that's what they call evolution. It is not an evolution, when we became bipedal and started being able to form a language. This hominid and Adam (a separate mental body) merged into a human being and the story of awareness began. Man left the kingdom of animals and started being aware of awareness.

And this is how the synchronization of my mental body, Adam (what we call soul), started synchronizing with my physical body, to become Homo sapiens. Nothing in the physical world changed at that time. Because at this point, it was not about change. It was a complete transformation of state and purpose. A quantum leap from the animal kingdom to the human one. This occurred instantly, so quickly, so subtly, that it wasn't noticed. Like a download on a computer system, nothing really happens immediately; the components of physical properties of the computer do not change. But the system behaves differently when the download is complete. And that night, for the first time, I had what I now know to be a dream. This never happened to me before, it disturbed me for a long time. But without sufficient words to describe it, or any abstract concept, I kept it to myself.

Abstract thinking is the idea which would take humans the longest time to understand, assimilate, and use. In the beginning, mental entities which we might call visions or apparitions introduced us to the concept of abstraction and taught us other things. Such non-human, non-terrestrial forms were clearly not composed of water, flesh, or any of the elements found on Mendeleev's chart. Call them angels, call them gods of mythology, but the fact that at that time, we could see them all, confirms their true existence. Each civilization had different versions of them. They stopped showing publicly to the collective less than 2000 years ago, when man learned to understand abstraction

They would come with humans, leaders that they would help spread wisdom, and to prove that these humans were not talking from illusion. They were here to back them up. And at the end of their mission they now appear as ideas from the Spirit/Truth world (i.e. chapter on Ether).

The first important lesson for mankind was the domestication of fire. The forests were ablaze due to climactic and natural events, and Homo sapiens observed that the flames frightened wild animals, many of whom preyed on man. Mankind understood then that fire could become a formidable defense against these wild beasts. In addition, fire warmed the air and left behind the roasted carcasses of animals. We dared to taste the charred bodies and learned that in many cases, the result could be pleasurable to our taste.

What an epiphany, to begin to think of the act of eating not merely as a necessity for survival, but to also associate food with pleasure and preference. While it wasn't exactly what we know as French gastronomy, the act of eating cooked meals had an impact on the digestive system of humans.

So here I am: Homo sapiens walking erect, using fire to keep warm, cooking food, and repelling enemies. Thinking abstractly about protecting my loved ones. And now ready for the next step: burying the corpses of others to show respect and honor.

There is a symbolism in the act of burial that was not immediately understood. Not only does it indicate intelligence by being concerned about bodily decomposition (and smell), there is the emotional component of recognizing the sadness experienced by loved ones. More abstractly, by burying the body in the dirt, we are giving back to the Earth what it has given us. These different dimensions of one act – practicality, respect, and symbolism – were representative of the intellectual and emotional advances of Homo sapiens, and prepared the species for the deployment of the universal morale code of humans.

Humans mainly lived on shores close to bodies of water, and learned how to travel on water with rafts. Huts near the shore would be built to provide shelter. But something happened to drive some humans further inland; unexpected tidal events and tsunamis forced settlements to go farther from the shore, up to the mountains, on a higher level. Rather than living in mountain caves as our prehistoric ancestors did, we reshaped the caves, and sculpted the mountains. The result was beautiful, and we realized that we could better control our environment to make beautiful residences and common areas.

Although some communities were migrator wanderers in search of safe territory as the seasons changed, most settled down to one area and began farming to produce food and textiles. We used the mountain terraces and open, flat fields. We domesticated some animals for food, fabric, or labor, and we became fixed in a specific geographic location. As an animal with sparse body hair, we would first use animal skins to emulate fur to keep us warm and protect some of our exposed body parts. Then, we learned to weave fabrics into clothes, which we learned to make aesthetically pleasing as well as functional. We extended this sense of aesthetics beyond clothing to dwellings, food, and ultimately to the development of art.

In their way, the mountains could be as dangerous as the shores and oceans. Our societies could be threatened by avalanches. The ground may not be stable enough or smooth enough to support the agriculture we had developed. So, we went to the plains which improved our ability to grow crops reliably and manage livestock effectively. A natural outcome of this, as certain individuals and families learned the lessons of the land better than others, was the concept of private property. Certain sections of the land would be farmed and managed by specific family groups, some with better results than others. And because agriculture is a multi-year endeavor – how one manages the property in one season can impact productivity in the next – it was natural to want to pass down the management of a particular plot of land to one's own family group, if the management was done well.

But even the plains can expose us to nature. Earthquakes. Tornadoes. Drought. And so our sense of society, of association with our kin and neighbors, became even stronger.

In the animal world, parents (and especially the females) provide their progeny lessons, food, and protection until such time as they are capable of independence; it is instinctive to teach and assist one's own children. But what is not necessarily innate or instinctive is the respect of parents and elders in general. Recognition of the elders' roles, and the care they are given once a certain age, is a learned behavior.

This was the next important human development: to recognize one's parents and other elders, and to acknowledge that a debt is owed to them even after achieving one's own independence. While intimate sibling relationships continued a little further in time, those with parents stopped completely and were considered forbidden. While it became understood that one had a responsibility towards parents when they reached a certain age, in all cases it was necessary to show them a certain respect.

Humanity had experienced great catastrophes: floods, tsunamis, avalanches, and earthquakes. We were starting to get to know planet Earth; we had experience here. The survival instinct resulted in social development and made us ready for the next step. Acknowledgement of our natural habitat is continual and never-ending, as is that understanding of the human condition which leads to our social morality and standards of behavior. Humanity exists to evolve, both physically and morally.

And this is the first part of our history. Where humans were on a survival mode. Getting to discover their bodies and their planets. Existing as a link in the food chain. Building the premises of the moral code. Gathering as much information as possible about the planet, what to eat, how to mate, how to calculate, how to do commerce, etc.

Today, one could easily register a feeling of disgust to the thought that our ancestors practiced incest, cannibalism, or human sacrifice. It seems that it has been a long way receiving our moral code, and the way has not always been straight and peaceful. Let's be empathic and compassionate towards our old selves. Perhaps humans from the year 3000 will look back at us with the same impressions, and will hopefully understand that we did our best with our actual level of awareness.

Perhaps the essence of humanity is our capacity to acknowledge and synchronize knowledge with behavior. The development of a universal moral code certainly takes a long time, and it seems to be an irreversible process and still is taking place through parliaments, human rights associations, and other organizations.

Beyond one's kin and associates in the community, there was a tendency among people to express worship and fear for deities or natural forces. Humans perceived a Sun God, a Wind God, a Rain God, a Lightning God, and a Moon God. Rather than recognizing these phenomena of nature as simply the result of the laws of physics, these phenomena were personified as Gods. In fact, the elite of society encouraged people to worship these personifications, built sculptures, and made offerings of some of their property, and most people did so. An era of cults, sects, and oracles devoted to one or another set of deities had begun. The people mainly lived on a survival mode, and were ready to abide to the elite for work, food, or protection. Differences between the cults led to wars. The manipulation of humans had begun, and might remain on Earth forever.

Temple's a way to associate the highest form of non-physical, prayer, and connection, with a tangible, dedicated space for communicating with the divine. At that time arose a current of thought (Abrahamic), the first rational skepticism. The recognition of the changing and transforming nature of all experiential objects that by definition could not be worshipped. Their ever-changing nature, by definition, could not make them a Creator to worship, as God by definition is never changing and never ceasing to be.

A little before that time, in the Hammurabi era, was set a written social and legal code. That has been later made more suitable and just for humans of that time, with the 10 commandments.

And then came the era of salvation. Not that monotheism appeared only at this time; it had appeared with the first Homo sapiens, but in a much simpler way. It consisted in the beginning of a recognition of a creator to worship, an invisible and subtle dimension and in the eternal nature of humans (existence before birth and after death). But as man evolved and lived in societies, every time he was ready to receive it, a new set of codes and laws were descended to him.

The succession of enlightened beings (with the help of non-physical beings in the beginning) bringing knowledge and more suitable behavior for mankind has stopped with what we wall "prophets." These people had one purpose (beside living their human lives), connecting humans to their true self and giving them guidance for how to live together and how to thrive easily during this journey on the physical plane.

Mostly, these codes were not to kill any form of life unless for food (certain type of animals) or self-defense against persecutors (humans who threaten other humans in a peaceful situation), and not to torture prisoners of war. To respect equitable exchange and agreements. To take care of orphans, widows, old or people with a handicap and to fight poverty.

To abolish slavery and not to make any segregation based on race, wealth, or origin, as the only difference between people is their behavior. To reveal and allow human dignity in each one. And other laws that completely make sense with our actual set of laws. They also said that these laws were inviolable, whether you believe or not in a Creator or an invisible world. And that is what we see today when looking back through history, and in modern times, there is a Universal Morale that is mirrored through legislation and law enforcement around the globe.

They obviously talked and shared their faith that there is one Creator, an invisible world, a before and an afterlife for all humans and that their information came from the Creator through Spirit. But it was made clear that in this area, it was human's choice and birthright to either believe it or not. And that's also what see throughout history and in our world today, a very large portion of the world believes in a Creator and choose to worship him in the tradition of its religion, whilst the rest do not and have (at least by law) the right to do so.

Living in groups, societies was human's fate. In the beginning it was the form of villages and then cities. I define a "village" as a group of people living under one unique current of thought. The Olympic village's purpose is athletes, the Bolshevik village's purpose is communism, the agriculture village is everything that has to do with farming and exploiting the soil. Therefor a village is based upon the unique party, thought, purpose. On the opposite there has been the concept of the city, which means the coexistence of different currents of thoughts, beliefs, philosophies and religions but ruled by the universal morale that is translated through laws established by people to enable life together for security (penal), practical (driving code), and other reasons.

Diversity in race, culture, and faith is the basis of the city "code." It is also ruled by the opposition in wealth, education, lineage, and knowledge, and that contrast is what causes expansion and deployment of a better world. In a period of crisis, forces try to get their people back into identity and separation for a short period of time (fascism), but the rule is that when crisis occur (social, economic, or otherwise) they actually are opportunities for taking the city to the next level of consciousness, leveling up the poverty line, taking care of our elders, orphans, and people with special needs, providing better systems for health and education.

Be it urban, rural, or wild, mankind will use nature's elements to build a home, and to nurture, and protect society's members. As any given society develops, the people in it adapt nature to facilitate communication, transportation, medication, and recreation.

To do all this requires transformation.

We learn how to transform elements of nature to ease mankind's interactions with it. We protect our bodies from the outside with fabric and with dwellings. We find edible things and transform them by refining them by cooking or preparing them.

The first manner of transformation is to use our physical bodies; our hands are tools for shaping, our feet are tools for moving. Later, we discover that we can shape more intricate tools, among which can be ways to improve on our hands and on our feet. To manufacture easier, or move or transport better or communicate faster with more efficiency. Until we discovered the steam machine that was really the precursor of industrialization. Bicycles, automobiles, trucks, trains, boats, planes. Now, man can travel to destinations both known and unknown, seeking more suitable places for self-development, expansion, or enrichment. Or simply to escape; to escape the limitations of the existing environment.

There is, however, a prerequisite for developing more sophisticated methods of transformation: communication. To interact and exchange ideas with other humans requires a common language.

A society begets a language. A language begets laws, which presumably clarify rules already being observed in the society. Laws beget a country, a formalized division of geography represented by flags and anthems.

Each society establishes its own norms on what is good and what is bad, what is beautiful and what is ugly, or what has value and what is worthless. Nature is not good or bad, beautiful or ugly, worthy or worthless; nature simply is.

Humans judge each other based on differences in wealth, status, appearance, acquisitions, and social relationships. But the most important and pervasive aspect of judgment is based on the individual's ability to be integrated within the norms and values of the society.

People group in communities, communities group in societies, and societies group in countries. All these groupings form a whole: humanity. And even humans sharing common physical traits can differ enough in culture and custom that it can be very difficult to unite them. Even within a common country, we perceive that the "other," when "different," could be a threat.

Everything man made with this raw material that is earth can be thought of as a human's physical manifestations, or the *here-below*. They can be applauded or denied. They form one of the rules of the game of life on earth.

A conversation with someone is a physical manifestation, turning fabric into clothing is a physical manifestation, the food

I am eating every day is a physical manifestation, the computer on which I type these words on is a physical manifestation.

Some achievements are an individual experience, others collective.

These results, these physical manifestations of mankind's efforts to manage his environment, are the main focus of his thoughts and ideas; he evaluates them continuously through his own review and his sense of the collective validation of these results. Mankind's attention is directed towards consistently analyzing and understanding the outcome of his achievements.

Both Mankind's collective results and individual results are effects, not causes; they are indicators of reality. The cause always lies in the mental realms, the creation, the collective and the individual ones. This section will be developed later in the Mental Realm chapter.

4.

TIME TRAVELLING TO MY PHYSICAL REALITY DESTINATION

There will come a day when the human race will extinguish by losing its habitation, which means Earth as we know it today will no longer be able to shelter us. That day will come before long, but we don't really know when. Because even if we combine our ability to predict projected, probable, possible, and fanciful futures, there will always remain this element of surprise, of which we have no idea yet. As when, the rendez-vous is very far in time, our current ceiling of knowledge is not enough to come up with a prophecy. One thing is sure, the day will come when the human's physical realm will vanish.

Humans already live on a debt mode with the resources of the planet. However, there seems to be an equilibrium that Earth tends towards. Humans will shortly be forced to be creative enough to completely transform most of their technologies, production systems, and most importantly, their modes of consumption. A new era is about to rise. Although I completely share the concerns of the environmental activists, the brilliant scientists and their reports, and the system reformists, I think that we are ready to enter a new level of consciousness beyond all what we knew up to now that will put in place new ways of going about life on Earth.

When I am talking about the loss of human's habitat, I am talking about the most probable scenario, an outer space object. A big asteroid will be sent to Earth, which will trigger the end of life on Earth as we know it today.

The universe, including today's Earth, is this environment conducive to the existence of the human being as such in this physical world. Homo sapiens knows that this is the environment where its appearance, its existence, its life, its evolution was made and is possible. The cosmic clock of the physical universe as it has been set, has a start and an end, which is not an appearance and a disappearance but more a transformation of energy and eventually of the state of matter. In the same way the start of experiencing our souls/mental bodies and the creation with a physical body in a physical world has a beginning and an end. We will transit to another form of consciousness and therefor cease our physical experience.

The era of man in these forms of physical bodies, in the realm of Earth and the skies with the present laws will come to end until their next transformation and transition in a whole new universe with a completely different set of laws, forms, shapes, etc.

As this has two levels to it, the last day of our existence on earth and the actual last day of this universe. I want to emphasize our departure from this realm, as we will not physically witness the end of the universe, just like we did not physically witness its birth.

An asteroid, which doesn't have to be as big as the one that fell on the dinosaurs' heads (12 km diameters) and ended their stay down here, will eventually fall on our heads.

Just a normal day on Earth, with humans who think that they have seen the worst and others, the best on Earth. Some empaths, and other rationally pessimistic people will feel it coming.

But even with all the knowledge that they have gathered and the incredible intelligence that they proved to have, they know that these events are very difficult to predict.

Vacant in their activities, walking in the streets, finding themselves in front of a cafe or with a camera interposed, recounting their lives, aspirations and problems. Humans who are in the illuminated part of the Earth will see a big ball of light crossing the sky. Those in the part where it is dark will see it too, but much brighter. No matter how awake or asleep, outside or inside a building, everyone will be frightened by the explosive sound caused by this stellar object crashing into our only physical habitat.

Certainly, some people will argue that humans will have already moved elsewhere, most likely Mars. But given the still fanciful nature of this idea, I prefer to address myself to those who will be on Earth that day. I am speaking of those who will physically witness this event.

The extinction of man will come from the fact that his dwelling will collapse or change shape (especially the biosphere) and will no longer be conducive to his life on Earth.

A few million years ago (geologists say 65 million years), an asteroid from the sky changed the face of Earth, and led to transformations on the latter, which allowed and made possible life form. And it is most likely the visit of another asteroid that will accelerate the destruction of the human habitat and the end of life on earth. I will ask my readers to keep this word acceleration in mind, as it is really a very important concept. By acceleration of the continuum, I mean a singular event, difficult (sometimes impossible) to predict, which blows up and cancels millions, sometimes billions of years, in the unfolding of the history of the universe and of man.

We don't really need to wait until we watch a science fiction movie to imagine that we are traveling on a spaceship through the cosmos that has obtained alien technology to create a biosphere inside the machine. We are already on a space-time vessel, which is a self-sustaining system, journeying around space, which is part of a (solar) system, which is part of a larger system, and so on. Each sub-system is an essential link in the upper system and vice versa. Our immediate system, the solar system, provides us with the energy necessary for today's living conditions. Comets and meteorites provide us with atoms of all kinds, minerals, gases, etc. And the beautiful stars make all kind of the raw material, the atoms.

A harmonious system that knows where it comes from and where it is going. That knows all the mechanisms implied. And that never fails at being and existing and doing and having and becoming what it should. Sharing all this information in a subliminal way to teach us its language, and reveal to us its secrets, until we are able to translate it in ours. Any small or large change in this system can drastically change the face of our Earth. But we can only see in a tangible way what our 5 senses and what our technology allows us to see; the rest we owe it to great minds who have gone to higher dimensions, often to bring back theories and sometimes experientable information.

Earth receives energy from the sun. Attractions and repulsions, forces with other celestial movements also create movement. Invisible threads between the various astral objects, including the Earth, stretch and distend creating a dance and therefore movements in this common sheet. The Earth participates just as well in this system and in turn sends particles, gas, and other matter. All the objects in the universe are interdependent, and the terrestrial activity has taken a more frantic pace since man sat on his throne, especially over the last 13000 years. Resulting in a bigger impact on the rest of the universe, which impacts us in return. A kind of echo game, which propagation would be interesting to measure by the study of the sounds it emits. It is undeniable that man created a kind of accelerated heartbeat of the Earth. Human activity on Earth is making her course faster and her heartbeat more intense, creating a complete transformation of ecosystems and eco-landscapes and therefore of the biosphere in general!

It reminds me of a little story. This is the story of a man I know who had acquired a piece of land (somewhere on Earth of course) not far from a rocky area, on a plain not far from the mountains. His land was a large plain where nothing grew, somewhat arid unplanted. There were a lot of stones. He had a vision for this relatively small piece of land. He wanted to plant it. He dug a well, then two, arrived at the water table then at the deep-water table. He built a basin to distribute the precious water in an economical and efficient manner, he removed what he could of the stones, and planted trees and then cereals. Before long, birds began to visit his land, the vegetation began to take shape and then bees came to join the party. As the people of the village saw that the land was taking shape and that the culture worked, they began to copy him. Before long, the autochthones domesticated goats, known for their small appetites and their ability to find food even on the slopes. Then sheep, cows, and poultry were brought too.

Thus, the landscape and the ecosystem were somehow transformed. But that's not all. A few years later, the rains became more frequent and the temperature became milder in the region. I can't help but extrapolate this example to Earth over the past few millennia. Little by little, man has modified the eco-landscapes and ecosystems, and therefore certainly the biospheres. Cloud formation is altered, the wind races the migration of birds, the reproduction of large animals and therefore their survival (often not in the face of sudden and rapid changes). There is no doubt that man's purpose is to control the climate on earth, no doubt. It's written in its code. And that's one thing that will allow Earth to remain that conducive environment as long as we exist on it. But when it comes to talking about powers as important as that of climate control, it goes without saying that we cannot deal with this subject locally, but rather globally because any modification in a place on Earth implies necessarily a modification everywhere else, even in an extra-terrestrial way. In short, most of the landscapes on Earth were shaped by humans. For urban, agricultural, aesthetic, or other reasons. But it goes further. Even some (young) mountains are deposits of human activity and not the result of plate tectonics. They will experience transformations and strata due to pressure, temperature, and other factors.

I'd really be curious to have a map of all of man's actions and modifications over the past 50,000 years, maybe 13,000 if that's too much. Not only on the plantation, the waters, and forests, but also on the marriage of species. All this shows how far we are from when man was frightened by nature, existing as a link in the food chain. Man, this being of nature who seems to have taken control of it. In a thoughtful, legitimate way? For how long? Still figuring out how to measure the impact of his actions. Only a dear 5th dimensional friend, meaning us in the future, can really tell us.

However, let's put a little discernment in our cup. Is man really this being above nature? Man seems sometimes to forget that he is physically the result of the latter, and that his survival depends on it. He also seems to have memory problems regarding the cataclysms that occurred on Earth.

Thus, in the continuum of Nature, the living always ends up

dying and the inert transforming. The universe, with its earth and its heavens, are doomed to their Big End. It can mean a crush at a point similar to that of the Big Bang, it can also mean a total transformation that we are not really able to imagine as the magnitude of the time elapsed is beyond our comprehension and therefore will inevitably include events which are done with the same laws but under different conditions.

The study and observation of the stars does not stop at describing their brilliance, their beauty or translating it into poems. People who study them want to know the conditions of their birth and disintegration. A star, a Sun, ends up and engulfing everything close to it before burning off. And in the normal continuum of things, this is precisely what is going to happen to our Sun and all of its system. We are then told that this event should happen in a few billion years. I tell myself a few billion years from now if time continues to flow the same way it does today, and if the Earth as we know it lives to this day.

However, in this long calm river of projections that we have on the future, there are always events that change the course of things. This is what I call acceleration in the course of events. Events similar to Armageddon that disturb and shake the arrow of time that some people tried to make.

The fall of an asteroid on the earth will spare us physically witnessing the end of the universe, as we were spared from witnessing its first steps, but we would most definitely be spectators of the following scenario:

The racing rock comes from the sky. It is the outstanding, startling, sound that is the most frightening. As soon as it passes through the atmosphere, you can hear its echo throughout the Earth. A kind of thunderous noise combined with the sound of a fighter plane in a loudspeaker that you would put in your ears. But that's just the beginning. The closer it gets, the strident, untenable, and extremely loud it gets. Our ears are not designed for these kinds of sounds. This is how it exceeds 280 decibels, 300 dB, it is humanly impossible to survive it, especially for people who will be close to its point of impact. Millions of people will begin to die before it even runs aground on Earth. On entering the atmosphere, it catches fire because of friction with the air. People who can look up will be able to see it, but most of them will be holed up, a survival reflex, and above all, an event that has no precedent in our history. Written history. Smoke and light in the sky.

Its course will not be random because the asteroid is attracted by its point of impact. A sort of magnetism. And Bang! it hits the ground and creates a tremendous shock wave, total destruction of everything it touches. The shock wave will spread through the oceans and cause tidal waves that will impact until the Moon's spiral movement! It's not nothing, it's not a normal day. From the moment it enters the atmosphere it starts killing humans, fauna, and flora. Everything is completely devastated or even destroyed. Earthquakes, tsunamis, volcanoes, unbearable sound, smoke (soot, dust, gas). An unknown and unimaginable vision will present itself to those present. Because, yes, there will always be human witnesses as long as man's stay on Earth is not over. From there, events follow one another, starting the complete and radical transformation of the ecosystem, the biosphere, the atmosphere, all will be affected. I like the saying it's not over until it's over. And believe me, that day will be the beginning of the end of our physical existence on Earth. Survivors (not much), those with higher survival skills, and who will be in areas where the instant effects of the asteroid will be less damaging, will most likely remain on Earth for some thousands of years more at a maximum. But saying on earth will seem like a metaphor, because it will be a whole different place. If not affected by the instant effects of this event, they will eventually be touched by the transformation that earth will know gradually. The here-below game will come to its end, and humans will be thanked for their stay in a body on Earth.

They will then go then, just like what happens to death people (i.e. next chapter), into a deep sleep for the lucky ones, and into more or less pleasant dreams world for others, awaiting their return, when the Earth will shine again with the light of creation and will be ready to welcome them. Again.

Yes, because in the meantime, there is a time when man is no longer a physical witness, perhaps the same duration that lapsed between the big bang and the appearance of the first man, it is not important at this level for man will not attend it, as he did not attend the beginning. He won't be back until the new universe, when finishing its transformation, is ready to welcome him again.

5.

WHAT ABOUT MY DEATH?

Eventually, the day comes where my story of a human being born into a physical body, interacting with a physical world, which both appears to and in "me" ends with physical death. Yes, I am leaving my avatar and with it, any capacity to feel or interact with the physical objects of this universe in a material way.

Any physical death of a human being is a cardiac arrest. A human being living in a physical body is an organism that breathes air. This process is carried out by a respiratory system whose motor organ is the heart. To be alive for a human being is to have this function performed. No matter the state of the respiratory system, no matter the state of the human organism (healthy or sick), no matter how this human being functions, even in a comatose state, to be alive is to breathe (inhale and exhale air). The first vital function of man, the most important and sine quinone one, to breathe. Once this function stops, whether the heart fails by disease, accident, or degradation, it means death.

Once born, man begins to breathe air, and dies when stopping doing so. In between, there is a long or short period of time called life on Earth, the here-below experience. Most of us don't really remember how we got here, but we know for sure that it was being born from a given womb. The other sure destiny is that we leave this reality when we die. A sure date, that haunts the lives of some, that others seem to never intentionally think about, and, which others are impatiently awaiting. The collective idea says that the likelihood of dying increases with age, but no one can really predict it for sure.

Babies, children, and young people die every day from neglect or accidents, from unknown or incurable diseases, or just from an organism that ceases to function correctly.

We have also all seen people of 90 or 100 years old who express themselves perfectly, who still function by walking, shopping, sometimes preparing to eat and for some, conveying us with wonderful knowledge and wisdom. Getting older seems to be a correlation, not a cause to effect factor to death. Thus, age is more of a component of the body's aging, traces of age on the use of different organs and components. It is the impact of the evolution, use, lifespan of the components of the human organism. It is also the impact that organs have on each other, and their ability to work together in harmony; a kind of communication between the different organs, and the modification of this last by wear, as well as the quality of the signals emitted by the neurological center and the rest of the human body.

For all that, can we say that a physical body that has aged well, that has been maintained in an optimal state, will not necessarily die? No. There are obviously people who keep their vital and nervous functions to their maximum potential without surviving the life reaper. So, we are born, we live in a more or less functional body, and we die. Aging impacts the quality of life in a body, but in no way prevents its natural or accelerated death. Everything that lives, is born and dies by definition. Death is part of life's cycle, man included. This passage between life and death is also a transition between the living and the inert. And if we look closely enough, the same atoms that make up the universe exist in the human body. Before birth, during our lifetime, and even after our death, atoms will survive our death and transform into something else. And It is the fact that these atoms hook and bond together in a certain molecular and then cellular way that make this organism arise. We would obviously add the "water" component element, inherent to all life form, but again, these are atoms that once came together.

The death of my physical body means that "I" lose my avatar. The avatar breaks down into atoms which turns into something else, organic matter, to make a tree or food for other living beings. The Earth takes back the physical elements it has lent me for a lifetime to experience a body and a world made of matter.

Our first physical experience with death is when another person dies. The body is most of the time buried underground, sometimes burnt, or in very few cases not found. Generally, we keep a physical location of the body, a grave marker or a jar to be still able to meet with the person, and this, in most of the cases, doesn't go further that 2 or 3 generation after the death.

It is difficult to detach from the physical image of a person. We keep pictures, memories in our head, and most recently, photos, even videos. Just like in a game, often as if removed, as if a thread had taken the person from the stage, from the play. And poof! One disappears from any physical interaction with us. Sure, we've been physically separated from some people before, but knowing that they can't play with us anymore is quite disturbing at times. It's weird.

Disturbing because, maybe we took certain people for granted in life, or when the person is "too" young. Perhaps we believe deep inside that physical death does not mean a person's mental body death. Questions arise, such as, *where is the person now? Can he/she see me or hear me?*

As if dead people were so real that they can't just disappear like that. Sometimes one has this deep feeling, an intuition that they still exist, but in another form. Even the most agnostic go through such states where they find it difficult to accept that this person has simply disappeared. So, some will visit their steles if they had the chance to have one, as a proof and acknowledgement of their passage on Earth, a kind of material landmark to feel and dialogue with them or their memories. And others will go further in their belief on an afterlife, believing (or knowing) that soon enough they will join them in the subtler universe. In the meantime, they can communicate by thought or prayer or just by accepting that their incarnational group ceases to exist, and go about their life.

No one never leaves this world for good, leaving the physical experience of this world does not mean leaving the universe.

Just like in this physical world, some people do not really come to realize a causal, mental, or emotional world. They do not understand the subtler dimensions of dreaming or deep sleep, and most people fail to conceptualize the afterlife. When someone dies most people don't know that this person still exists but has only lost their physical body, which does not make them less existing "here and now" but in more subtle realities. It is true that this will only concern people who have faith (or for others with an intuition at the very least) in the existence of subtle dimensions which we will try to discuss in other chapters.

CHAPTER 2

THE INVISIBLE WORLDS

1.

"I" GETS AWARE OF EMOTIONS

Of all the tools that I have been given, the most ancient and powerful one is emotion.

Emotions allow me to perceive, understand, and interact with the world in a subtler way than with the five physical senses.

I can feel when something affects me positively or negatively, when my attention to an object triggers a good or a bad feeling. By object, I mean any stimuli: a thought, a conversation, something visual; any experience or situation of my inner and outer environment.

How subtly an emotion affects me can make it very difficult to define or conceptualize exactly what the properties of emotion are. It is a very subjective and personal experience; yet each of us, individually, experience emotions.

As soon as I arrived on the planet, I experienced the two basic emotions: feeling good, as opposed to not feeling good.

When I am fed, clean, rested, and cared for, I feel good. I am happy. I smile. I laugh. Or perhaps I simply sleep peacefully. When hungry, dirty, in pain, or unsafe, I am not feeling good; I cry. A baby's emotions are very simple and are very easy to decode.

A baby does not yet intellectualize the rise of or the display of emotions. There is no inappropriate time, place, or situation as far as a baby is concerned. Without any social mask, a baby is genuinely, naturally his or herself, expressing its pure emotional state of the moment. The outward expression of how a baby is feeling is always directly linked to its inner and outer conditions and its immediate physiological needs. The mind develops with age, but the emotions are born with the baby in their pure, perfect state, and give at each moment an effective signal to the actual situation.

As I begin interacting with adults, I learn to understand them better, and I realize that their emotions operate on a wider spectrum. Like light being fragmented though a prism into a variation of colors, so too, can the basic emotions be fragmented. From the basics of "feeling good" and "feeling bad," emotions are refined into joy, sadness, anger, despair, excitement, or fear.

Just as how we perceive and react to the physical world being passed through a filter of validation, our emotional state is analyzed and compartmentalized into what is acceptable, and what is not. Over time, we process how to exhibit our emotions outwardly according to the situation. We establish a grid of which expressions of emotion are appropriate in what context, depending on whether the relationship we have with the observer is professional, financial, romantic, familial, and so on.

Some expressed emotions are seen as normal, others exaggerated or overdramatic. We see some emotional reactions as symptomatic of a psychological imbalance. Each society seems to agree on which emotions can be exhibited to others according to the circumstance. In some societies, if you are not seen to openly mourn the death of a family member, you are seen in a negative light; while in other societies, the bereaved is expected to be composed in public and mourn only in private.

Later in life, I realized that some seem to exhibit a deeply emotional state for no apparent reason. When I first saw this and asked about it, I was astonished that when asked, a person would answer, "I don't know what is happening to me! I don't know! Stop asking me!" Perhaps I expected that a person – any person – should know and be able to explain and retrace their emotions. It was as if this person has mastered the art of activating any emotion on demand (like an actor who can vary their role from villain to victim in different films, and exhibit the consequent varying emotions). Or, as if they are disconnected from their "selves" to the point that they seem unable to trace the origin of the emotion and the events leading up to it.

Perhaps such a state is rooted in childhood experiences which have been repressed, and then new events cause recollection. Acknowledging these patterns and shedding light on them is essential to understanding the human emotional condition. Yet, the question remains: how far should one go, and for how long, to try to heal all these wounds and blockages? In such a short life, should we spend our present healing our past in an attempt to fix the future? When is one really going to live? Isn't there a more direct path?

Alternatively, such behavior may simply result from a habit of mind; one gets used to a certain feeling, owns it, and makes it a behavioral blueprint. The person develops a loyalty or commitment to a particular character trait or emotion, to a persona that took a significant time to build up – a persona with which they now identify.

Eventually, this creation, resulting from unwanted or uncontrolled feelings and frozen in time, is recognized to be only the result of a disconnection from the natural emotional system detection, which is otherwise always accurate. The person loses the ability to experience that truest part of their nature which helps them understand why, when, and how emotions emerge.

In early stages of life, emotions are attached to the current situation – to physical experiences, such as hunger or pain, interaction with the immediate environment, such as a toy or other people, or internal personal experiences, such as a thought or a dream. Sometimes it would only take an image in one's head to trigger a particular emotion. At that time, it would only require me, for example, to remember a horror movie, and I would find myself in an uncomfortable emotional place. Adults would explain that the images bothering me were not real, but my body and mind could not meaningfully tell the difference.

In the course of growing up, a child, with the help of its environment, transforms simple emotions into feelings frozen in time. They are used to subconsciously building an association between facts, events and feelings, a habit to feel a certain way in certain situations. This can override the immediate trait of the emotional signal.

For instance, if at age 6 someone is trying to abuse me, I cannot do much about the situation. As a result, the instinctual signal I receive generates fear and tells me to run away, but my actual circumstance keeps me from doing so. Later in life, if I do not regain control of or make peace with my guidance system, I may react as a victim when faced with a dangerous situation (and maybe stay in it), which I may in fact be able to control or leave.

Such reactions very often become a handicap to our mental faculties and their efficiency. Our learned, repetitive associations between ideas, people, behaviors, and places, as well as the feelings they have generated in us in some sense cripples us, and makes our protective instincts less reliable. The pattern does not take into consideration the actual situation.

Those who function like this will revisit these feelings in these situations due to a fear of losing the identity they have constructed. They are concerned that a change in behavior will betray their loved ones, or will challenge what they know of the human experience. Society often defines its members in accordance with a certain scale of emotions which they have historically exhibited.

Emotions become linked to beliefs. As the mind evolves, each event creates a belief which is attached to and tainted by the emotion invoked at the time of the event. Memory then associates this emotion with future similar events.

So, what we come to know as success, happiness, joy, love, or hate becomes directly linked to events, or the nature of an event. We create social expectations for how each event should make the person feel, which may be at odds with the actual emotion generated by each event due to childhood experiences.

Our original emotional signals stay forever pure and neutral, never containing more than two states: I feel good, or I don't feel good. Building upon this base, tainted by feelings created or adopted, we become disconnected from this essence. The emotional signal or system remains a very important tool, maybe one of the most important tools to answer important questions like:

How does it make me feel to think about this? To live this situation?

Deeper questions might follow, for those interested in understanding more about themselves:

What belief made me have this association? Is it a valid belief that is true all the time, everywhere? Is it a general truth?

If I am not feeling good, for instance, if I am feeling pain because I have a toothache, we can expect that the emotion is pure and relatively true. But if I am not feeling good because I think that based on some recent event, all humans are disloyal, the desperation I feel is likely an extrapolation of earlier events in my life. Studying the emotion in these terms, in a sort of cleansing exercise, could be beneficial as it has an instant impact on our self-awareness, and speaks volumes about the power of the mind.

Understanding and cleansing these uncontrolled or preconceived feelings helps in avoiding or correcting addiction to certain emotional states (like constantly seeking a euphoric state that has nothing to do with happiness through some experiences, or being in a constant melancholy that has nothing to do with actual daily life challenges or worries).

Consciously or subconsciously, man pursues an ultimate happiness that would lead to inner peace. Indeed, from an early age, infants grasp the idea of the two emotional states, and seek to feel good by engaging in activities that have historically created the "good" feeling in them. They recognize that certain objects trigger this good feeling. These objects evolve and change as the infants age and new centers of interest are found, but the basic emotion remains the same.

Before long, infants understand that adults want to please them and will try to provide what is asked for. But the day comes when, having decided that some requests or demands cannot or should not be accommodated, the adults answer with a "No." The child, accustomed to getting whatever they asked for, resents this change in behavior, and thinks, "One day I will be an adult and will get what I want by myself. I just need to grow up, that's the key." The child will often believe that they can overcome the obstacles which the adults have said prevent the realization of their desires.

Some chase euphoria, confusing it with happiness, by the acquisition of exterior objects: powerful cars, perfect families, a soul mate, the latest fashions, a higher education degree, and so on. Others have stopped pursuing anything, repressing their desires due to repeated failures, or fearing that acquisition will not bring fulfillment. A dream unfulfilled is seen as failure, and the fulfillment of a dream could lead to disappointment. Was all that effort worth it in the end?

While there is "feeling good" and "not feeling good," another state exists, one I rarely encountered in my life up until 3 years ago. This is a void state, where emotions don't seem to exist. Think of a moment when you were in deep concentration, or when you are weary from exercise, or when meditating.

From a very young age, a child realizes that it is pleasant to feel good, and learns what action is likely to lead to that state. Certain people, certain experiences, evolving with age and interest, enable the achievement of a pleasant feeling.

To summarize, emotions are born with the baby; they are a signal that gives a diagnostic of the current situation, a sense through which subjective reality is perceived. Over time, the basic emotions evolve into more complex feelings, which are often reactions to subconscious conditioning and past experiences and associations.

An emotion can also be an indicator as to the origin of a thought. The excitement that is born with an idea suggests that the person wants to pursue this idea. A feeling of fear indicates that the idea should be abandoned.

Empathy is encouraged in our society; we are expected to try to understand people's feelings. Compassion is a high virtue which enables us to interact positively with others. But we can never truly feel what another person is feeling. Emotions seem simple, but they are not; they contain much information which is not easy to translate. One has to be aware that, contrary to our other senses, emotions are very personal. Emotions are manifestations of an inner communication. The less a person lets their past trauma influence their feelings, the purer the signal is and the clearer the inner communication will be.

2.

THE EMOTIONAL DIMENSION

The emotional plane, often called the astral plane, is directly linked to consciousness, where all logic is challenged. Emotion is indeed an object, therefore a form of communication independent of any mental activity. Understanding, intellect, reasoning, or logic have no place in it; they have no meaning in this space, and therefore cannot function. It is a primordial world compared to the universal and human mental plane (as discussed in the next chapter). It's a world of sensations and feelings, a much subtler form of communication. The subtlest form of communication between reality and the human being is that of emotion. Here is the first objective plan, the first experience.

Such a world of emotions is the canvas on which all emotions are expressed. They are sensations, images, scenes, sounds, melodies, lyrics, symbols of all kinds, colors, entities and more. Here, the possible knows no limits or filters. There is no concept of good and evil, there is neither true nor false.

Here exists pure feeling, a translation of emotions that goes from the ugliest monster to the prettiest unicorn. Anything is possible and everything is allowed, because on this plane no laws of the mind apply yet. Welcome to The Fantasy World. As if consciousness gave way to all potential outcomes, probabilities, possibilities, fantasies, and dreams, to flourish before processing, giving them a form and a framework of laws in the mind. In other words, the decision has not yet been taken at this level. That's why, on a human level, intuition must be acknowledged, even while we apply the lessons of the mind before acting.

This emotional, instinctual space, a conceptualization of all the emotions that exist, can be thought of as a dimension with floors or levels, where each level represents the experience of a given emotion. There are no boundaries between floors; like an elevator going up or down from one floor to another, but the borders between floors are blurred. There is a multitude number of stages, and therefore of vibrational fields to which we connect when we visit this place. We visit here through the only key possible, the emotion of the moment.

This place is visited in a perceptual way during our "dream" state of consciousness. In a dream, I can visit both the mental and astral planes; sometimes when receiving a clear message, I enter each of the two, one after the other. This emotional world can also be visited in a waking dream conscious mode, when my mind wanders, or when I experience particular situations. We might have a sense of "Deja-vu" (already seen), or a strong intuition, or a sudden inexplicable emotional twinge; these are personal because they are subconscious experiences. Such experiences cannot really be explained, rationalized, or proven to others, and getting the input or interpretation of others is not in any event their purpose; these are internal communications. And, this place is also visited on a daily basis in my waking state in the form of feeling that can cause, when strong enough, a sensation in my body.

It is of course possible to talk about such experiences, like if we want to know how experts on human psychology might interpret the symbolism involved, or how friends who know us well might see the imagined events. We might narrate our experiences in such cases as a story, from which we sometimes might seek the moral; more often we would just share our amazement at what we saw there, which the mind does not quite understand. The download is done systematically, information automatically captured by the subconscious.

Some have shared with the world their memories of these virtual hanging gardens, making the echo of this dimension heard through works of art. The grandeur and diversity of this plane has reached us here in the physical world through these geniuses, great artists who bring us back melodies, paintings, literature, poetry, and even mathematical equations.

Such works of art, such visions into the astral plane, seem to stop all mental and scientific activity because such activity cannot explain the phenomena of beauty, love, or aesthetics. They do not even seem to belong to this physical world. They are alien to other forms of perceiving our world. And yet, it is this emotional world which is the first object that diverts our attention from that which is certain.

The astral plane is full of things that were, things that are, and things that will become; but most of its contents have never seen the light of day, and never will. Everything present in this space is the sum of everything conceivable in thought or achievable in action. However, not everything will manifest in reality, for that is not the purpose of this astral plane.

There is, of course, more than beauty and magic in this space. There are levels in this dimension, as mentioned earlier. At the bottom of the metaphorical abyss is a dark, sad, slow, heavy world, to which visitors gravitate based on their dominant emotion of the moment – impotence, depression, frustration. In such low places, the visitor has the impression of being chased, of falling, of being trapped, of being unable to seek help, of being threatened by strange creatures. Or when awake, of being persecuted, judged, or hated.

But as one's active emotional state advances and progresses to more positive states such as contentment or hope, it tends not to regress to lower floors; one perceives more beautiful scenes, more shimmering landscapes. The emotional lift continues to progress, feeding on its own growth, advancing and giving us access to the highest spheres of this plane. Images, symbols, and feelings are more pleasant, carrying positive messages. They are signs which only the subconscious receives, as only the subconscious is able to understand the language and decode any meaning found in the messages on this plane. Receiving messages is not the only purpose for visiting this plane. Sometimes, the purpose is simply to give us a positive affirmation, a moment of respite or rest from reality. It can be a restorative, curative way to heal certain emotional wounds which may have left traces on the mental or physical body. The emotional body knows only the present moment and therefore has no memory to cleanse. The visit to the astral plane, or "dreamland" may simply be a nice event, a bonus, offered as a recreational gift for the simple pleasure of enjoying it.

3.

"I" RECOGNIZE MY MENTAL BODY: THE MIND

At my arrival on Earth, I was a newborn with no objective knowledge or understanding of my physical reality. I was warmly welcomed by those already here with joy and open arms. "Here is a new program on Earth," they said. "We will do our best to make it the best version possible of itself."

I come from a particular womb, into a specific family, under a given flag, with an established and inherited citizenship, religion, and language. All I know and am taught is part of a local and national culture.

I was given a name, an identification code to recognize and reference me.

I didn't know the name of things at birth; in fact, I didn't even know "things" objectively. I had no frame of reference, nor experience of life on Earth.

Many entities will be involved in my learning, my human apprenticeship; they will relay to integrate and prepare me to live on Earth. I am this white page, a blank canvas upon which will be written everything that I capture as I explore my environment.

From my first weeks on Earth, whenever I would detect a new object in the palette of my experience, I would point my finger towards it, and perhaps even reorient my body. I would fixate on it, observe it, and when possible, get close to it. I would get an urge to hold it, to put it in my mouth, to cover it with all my attention, to become one with it, to know it in its essence. At that stage, I didn't really understand that I have five different and distinct senses. My attention, my ability to concentrate and study, was what enabled me to identify and, later, to recognize every object.

Those who have preceded me in this time-space reality already have much knowledge, and take time to share with me. They are installing in me the software, the parameters, the program of life on Earth.

Adults were very excited to teach me everything: names, definitions, purposes, concepts of those things which they believed were important for me, so that I could survive, evolve, and perhaps thrive in their community.

It is not just when I point to an object that they educate me about it; sometimes they would call my attention to something. They would show it to me, then repeat its name until I understood. They might show me how to use something, as well as how not to use it. They use repetition to teach me, and with patience it is a method that pays off. I also mimic them all the time, attracted to some, repelled from others. I tend to build my "acting" skills, as I want to become an adult.

I am given between six months and a year to learn how to form words. The elders will explain things to me with love and patience until I am about two years old. I notice that adults, in general, love me as a baby; they want to teach me something, to play with me, to hug and kiss me. They cannot wait to see me communicate with them in manners rather than pointing, crying, or groaning.

After this first two years or so, adults go to a higher level of teaching. They go beyond teaching me the names and uses of the most important common objects, to lessons on proper behavior, manners, and hygiene. I begin receiving their truths on the difference between what is good and what is bad, virtue and vice, success and failure codes.

In other words, I am being educated in life and its rules.

Sometimes, adults start their sentences with things like, "You'll understand when you get older" or "Life is a serious matter, you can't just take it easy," or even "I am doing this for your own good." Once, a teacher even said to me, "If you don't listen to me, you'll end up selling peanuts on the street." It wasn't too clear why selling peanuts on the street was a bad thing, and years would pass before I understood what she meant.

Yes, kids ask many questions, too many. As a child, I wanted to know everything about anything that I encountered in my explorations. The poor adults, not always having the right answer or sufficient time, would often take shortcuts in responding to my insistent requests. They would repeat what they heard elsewhere. They felt obliged to respond even to questions they could not answer, because they did not want to lose this opportunity to continue to be my primary information source. They feared the possibility that I could get information elsewhere which challenged their own belief systems; they feared losing the opportunity to raise me in their image and within their own framework.

I learned that there were some taboo subjects, and when I broached these topics, I would be told that I am too young to know. The adults seemed disturbed that I asked such questions, even scared, and they would follow up with a question of their own: "Where have you heard about that?" But their reactions and statements never stopped my curiosity. By intuition, I felt all the answers for all the questions of the universe should be available to everyone and anyone.

It has to do with thoughts…

Parallel to the life of our five physical senses is a realm of the invisible; intangible things started to develop inside my mind. It began through conversations with adults, or sometimes through things which I overheard. I might also be exposed to things through films or television. Many stories are told to a child; facts about events that occurred when the child was not physically present, and often events which even the storyteller has learned secondhand.

Sometimes what I am told are imaginary tales, fantasies, often metaphorical, intended perhaps to teach me something, to convey a moral, to entertain me, or to help me sleep. All these stories in truth had a moral behind them, and subtly anchored a belief in my mind. I might learn from Snow White that stepmothers could be monsters.

This invisible, intangible world of thoughts and ideas consists of what has or may have happened, but which I have no direct experience of. Mimicking my elders, I build this imaginary realm; a world where all things are possible, which exists even beyond my own experiences. I reinforce this muscle of imagination every day. Later, though, I begin to understand that this realm, too, has its own rules, its own truth and deceptions. Much of what is described is not in the physical world, and I notice that adults often contradict themselves when they say that something is not possible.

With all this in mind, let's return to my attempt to describe the human mind, and find the right words to properly describe this very important tool. After the five-physical senses and the emotion sense appears the seventh: Mind. I have always lived with this tool, but I have only recently discovered it. But this is not the beginning. It all started in the Universal Mental Creation Realm.

4.

THE UNIVERSAL CREATION REALM

I, the mental realm, am not the first object to exist (astral world), but I precede any sensible world, sounds or material forms. I am prior to any physical manifestation, my "matter" equivalent. Perhaps, then, I can be considered the origin, so much sought after by scientists. Transcending the Planck wall, the Big Bang, and any manifested (hi)story of the universe.

I am the dimension in which everything was thought, in which everything was organized, planned, and decided. I am the plan for the cause which consequence will be the physical materialization unfolding of everything.

After dreaming, imagining, allowing all possibilities and scenarios, a decision was made. This final decision of the chronological deployment that is actually going to happen, is called "the Creator will."

The first Creation was a space and its components, Earth and the heavens. The idea, the concept of thought form. That will be the realm of creation. Then time was created, which is the deployment mechanism (duration, chronology, dates, cycles, gestation, rhythm, order) that allows our mind to go backward and forward to understand these concepts. Then were created the laws that would play in the architecture and the building of these elements. There has to be objects before laws that govern these objects and not the other way around. There has to be cars, then a code to drive these cars. And finally came the intelligent localized, separate entities (spirit bearers, mental polarity bearers, animals, and humans).

Space, Earth and the heavens were the abstract surface of the creation with boarders, the sum of locations (space coordinates), and dimensions or realms (astral, mental, physical and others) that can be thought of as layers and that densify (from the subtler to the more sensible). Densities also mean level of awareness of knowing and understanding the different realms. An object can appear in one or many dimensions depending on its ability (the access level it was given) to densify and on its will (intentional choice) to visit them or not.

Space is, at the same time, the container, and is also the raw material for the appearance of its content. Meaning that space modulates itself to give birth to an object. The most common example are clouds; they are objects that appear in the sky which they are part of. It is an object which can become objects. It becomes a content by a transformation mechanism, which becomes a modulation of its inherent nature through the mechanism of time.

Please bear with me here, I want to make it clear that I am not making a description of the actual, physical space. I am still talking about the "idea" form in the Creation realm. But as you will discover it later, in the Creation realm there is no real difference, as the concept and the material object are perfect replicas of each other. There is never a bug in the system or a disparity between the image and the physical reality.

Time remains a mental activity. We see its fingerprint on physical objects (their evolution, transformation) and so thinking is the mirror of time. Man has become aware of this fundamental concept thanks to natural phenomena. The revolution of the Sun and the Moon that produce the alternance between daytime and nighttime form together the first unit: one day. The recurrent moon cycle sets the month unit, then seasons reveal themselves and with them the year unit (this helped building calculus in human minds, but that's another subject).

Another phenomenon that helped with inputting time in the mind of humans is death. Death gives each one of us a certain passage of cycles on earth, a certain duration of time spent of this realm. Both the cosmic phenomena and the death phenomenon taught man that time features durations, cycles, gestation, rhythms, chronology, dates, etc. From a human perspective, as it is experienced differently by other life forms and inert forms. Time is the byproduct of thinking. Thought happens in time; the physical reality only knows and experiences the here and now.

The Creation Plane is the plane of the beginning of the experience. It is well ordered, well thought out, a world of objects representing what total awareness had decided to achieve. Immanence or transcendence is not yet clear. The bridge between total awareness and the conscious decision of a Creation is the fruit of this intention combined with a will.

The plane of concepts emerges. The Creation mental plane begins. When I refer to pure consciousness, I mean the source of everything that is: the Creator.

This plane of universal creation is equivalent to the plane of pure mental activity; thought and decision occur here first. This means having an intent, deciding on a vision, designing the objects to help realize that vision, then giving function to everything in its deployment. Laws of natural behavior are put in place. Desire, intention, decision, vision, will, design, overview, total omniscience, control, government, infallible laws, chronology, and relative time merge in the here and now. While everything exists from start to finish simultaneously in this plane, the deployment is chronological; the cycles and durations are respected. And the revealing of its content is done to the creation of entities (man included) as they go in the scenario. For their awareness longs to be one with the Creator awareness. Everything, every concept and object, exists at the same time but does not happen or reveal itself at the same time to the created.

From a human perspective we cannot see or experience this realm with our five senses at the same time. In the physical world, I cannot be in both prehistoric times and the Renaissance simultaneously. Where does the past go after the events have occurred? It returns to the Creation mental plane. And where is the future before its events have been realized? They remain in the Creation mental plane.

Please keep in mind that we are not talking about the future in the human sense of the term, meaning where I would be at age 54. These are information that are in the human mental plane (i.e. human mental plane chapter). We're referring to the physical future of the objective universe; how did energy materialize in an expanding universe? What will happen when the Earth disintegrates? What will happen when the sun is dead? How will the next universe look and what will be its laws?

The emergence of this mental plane means that the notion of time (chronology, duration, cycles, and gestation) has manifested, has come into existence. The Creation mental plane is the first object, the first creation of the total awareness (the source of everything), and on this plane are superimposed all the other planes, the human plane in particular.

The source is experienced, and realized in the world of the object. Meaning total knowledge is allowed to be tangible. It starts with an intention, an imperative statement: BE! And it WAS. You might call this realm a prophecy fulfilled in advance; once the intention is expressed, the initial and final images drawn, then the creation process begins.

Once created, this universe needed codes, laws, and outlines. The creation process consists of thinking about the components of the prophecy, then drawing the details and outlines until they take form and shape. Planning the gestation durations, the cycles, the evolution of everything, birth and annihilation, recycling by the whole. Each element – each electron, atom, or cell had encoded in it its own laws and natural forces. For instance, gravitation, repulsion, and polarity were put in place. Each entity was thought about, and decided if made with material or non-material elements, when it would appear (transforming from a prior state) and disappear (transforming to a next state) and what role should it play in this whole.

Other natural laws are established for the physical realm: the principle of conservation of energy (nothing is created, nothing is lost, everything is transformed; the principle of cause and effect), for example. Or, the law of non-contradiction for the human mind. Other codes govern the chronology of events, restricting the superposition of related phenomena and making possible projections and realization by the human mind of what was and what will be (intra and extrapolation). Perhaps most importantly is the concept of the etheric realm, wherein resides the energy for what is to always be available.

The end result of all this was the creation of a mental spiritual world, a form-thought model of Earth, the heavens, the laws governing this reality and its inhabitants; call it the "code" by which and in which we live.

So, the time of the inhabitants, created entities, came. It came first of a mental body form, then later of a physical one (life form, animal kingdom), and unexpectedly, humans (which would include all forms).

The first entities of a mental nature that have been created were the spirit bearers. And by spirit (i.e. chapter on Ether), I mean, governing laws, valid, relevant and true information (thoughts, ideas, concepts). the guarantors of the deployment of the plan. In other terms, positively charged thoughts.

Then came about duality entities, having access to both true and false, valid and futile, relevant and illusory realities, recognition and denial. This was the first introduction to a kind of free will, only applicable to thought form. These entities were therefore carrying both "positive" and "negative" charges. Although, initially, the concepts of "positive" and "negative" really do not apply; things merely happen, and the implementation of concepts such as time and design are done automatically. There is no contrary force, in the sense that the mental model takes shape gradually, over what will come to be known as "time."

And as the physical universe, the Earth and the skies were drawing and revealing, the creation added other entities, physical ones: life form, animals, insects.

Once the first particle of matter was born from energy, there emerged vibrational equivalent thoughts with negative charges. This helps us understand the duality of nature, as matter (in the form of atoms and molecules) cannot exist without a negative charge. Positive is not in opposition to negative; they work together in the construction of the final image for the benefit of everything. Each developmental stage of the event is greeted with fervor, enthusiasm, and amazement as the dimension approaches the final destination of its configuration.

A mental entity living in the universal mental plane is not systematically aware of itself, nor of the rest of existence. This plane is, in that sense, the perfect replica of the physical world wherein I can exist as a human and live in Los Angeles, yet have no idea that Tokyo exists. Only pure consciousness is omnipresent and omniscient at each level.

Having clarified that, let us now consider other entities inhabiting the universal mental plane.

The sky, the Earth, the cosmos; mountains, trees, and animals, are all entities of the universal mental plane, but do not have the option of being aware of their consciousness. They simply ARE. Nor do they have what we know as free will. Their existence is a happening, an effect of the occurrence of specific conditions in a certain chronological path. In a sense, they decide to exist.

Eventually, the source introduced a new element, one which was an entity in the universal creation mental plane, but also had its equivalent on the physical plane. A humanoid, initially closer to a wild beast living on the physical plane on Earth, developed the capacity for ideas, thoughts, awareness, consciousness to all concepts and to awareness to be aware, and until then, had been restricted to entities in the mental plane. Other entities in the mental plane were astonished. Up until to that point, mental entities had no physical equivalent; they remained in the state of ether which was considered to be much more noble than any other element. Positively charged entities asked how a being of matter could have its own mental body and therefore be able to navigate in, and be aware of, both planes of existence and more.

The humanoid had flesh and was perishable, requiring nourishment, capable of killing, and transparent in the sense that all his actions were obvious. It was an animal, yet in contrast to what were considered universal laws, was aware of the entities on the mental plane. Positively charged entities wanted to understand, even though they knew that ultimate truth was inaccessible to them; they were not omniscient, and were only aware of what was revealed to them. Negatively charged entities rose in indignation, feeling humiliated. They had never had an equivalent in the mental realm, let alone in the physical one. Their positive thought counterparts had no impact on them, since they were not seen as a danger, but rather a counterbalance.

In contrast, negative thoughts were deemed the sworn enemy of the human mind; harboring such thoughts would have bad consequences on the human physical world. The bearers of the spirit (and by spirit, I mean laws, valid information, and conscious knowledge of objects), have the mission of directing and bringing the law and elements which they have been asked to give to the different elements of the objective reality. Spirit bearers carry only the positive charge and are therefore completely subject to the will of the Creator. They do not have their own free will in their mental body.

Spirit bearers therefore only have one option to use in this plane. In humans, they will manifest themselves in thought: inspired thought, intuition, discovery of physical laws, composing a musical melody. We might think of such thoughts as downloads. Some human beings download such manifestations (using currently unclear parameters) into concepts in the physical reality and share the result with other human beings.

Besides the spirit bearers – always the positive entity – the alternative is the polarity entity, having both positive and negative options. It also has no physical equivalent and exists only in the world of thought, but it is a thought more of interaction and inception. In other words, it may interact with different mental bodies in different ways, suggesting variable ideas to them.

Having lived the first part of its mental world existence with entities without polarities (ores, rocks, animals, and even bearers of the spirit), negative thoughts could only start to manifest when humans receive their individual mental plan; mankind is the first mental and physical entity to have choice and polarity.

Of course, the human being (or mankind, as we know it today), must first pass through the humanoid stage before it receives a mental body, more commonly called 'Adam.' We will come back to this later.

The universal mental plane was created objectively. To understand if an object of reality belongs to this plane, we apply a certain methodology. We ask, is it a universal truth, an element that can be experienced in the same way no matter the point of reference, an element that resists a change in its reference point?

For instance, death. Death is an element of the universal mental plane. Whatever one's point of view, geographic location, current of thought, skin color, religion, genetic tendencies, or financial capital, the physical body will die one day.

Other such examples include the sun (by whatever name given to it by the different cultures on Earth), the sky, trees; these are elements written in the universal mental plane, primordial to the human mental plane, and therefore resist any change in point of view.

Many have theorized whether or not what we know as reality is in fact an illusion or simulation, a product of our imagination, but the universal truth of the mental plane can shatter such theories. The fact that this realm exists, regardless of changes in perspective or point of view, should be sufficient proof of its universal truth as observed and experienced by anyone not weak-minded or suffering from delusions.

Let us keep in mind an important distinction: we are enumerating the specifics of the universal plane, and not of the human mental plane. We will consider the latter in a different chapter, and consider how, because it is an extension of creation, it may be considered a creation itself.

This universal, or creation plane, has another trait: it can be thought of as an inescapable prophecy which comes true. It unfolds as and when conditions necessary for each phenomenon are met. What we call the principle of cause and effect implies a primordial cause for each effect, a rational explanation for each event or behavior. More frequently, it is not a single event or condition, but the simultaneous occurrence of several, resulting in a new effect. A tree doesn't merely "grow." Rather, the combination of a seed, soil, water, sunlight, and minerals in the proper conditions and temperature leads to the emergence of a tree.

Think of the universal mental plane as a container of the intention, of the will to transform the initial components, under the expected conditions, into the final realization of the vision. The container encompasses the quantity of finite but necessary energy the vision requires, the laws necessary for the sequential execution of the plan, the name of each object resulting from the vision, the sound linked to it; the object's birth, death and transformation. It is the container of all global and total knowledge of vision, where the visionary, creator, architect, designer, innovator, and originator are one: The Source.

Such a plan was created for the design of natural material objective reality, but the concepts can be used as building blocks for other dimensions.

Once all objects had been drawn, visualized, and named, laws were needed to govern the movement, interaction, and evolution of the object; its unfolding from primordial moment, where it was total energy in its pure state, to its final image and state. These laws are affirmations: irreversible, immutable, put in place from the beginning. These are laws, but unlike the laws of men, which can be sidetracked and breached subject to a penalty, they are operating laws, irrefutable orders essentially inscribed into each component of the universe. They establish standards of action and reaction, and apply beyond and outside of the consciousness of everything. They simply ARE.

The irreversibility of events is also a law, because no moment can be experienced twice; the laws apply at each moment, to each state uniquely and distinctly. It was a great relief to understand this when I was following the CERN collider experiments. Although I was amazed by the technology and discoveries, I wondered if, by attempting to reproduce the primordial events of our universe, even in a slight way, we would end up counterbalancing the equations and thus create chaos. But nothing, no action, will ever be able to modify the global trajectory of the universe, nor disrupt the chronological arrow in which it was launched. At best, we will more about our physical world; at worst, we might trigger a volcano or earthquake, or a temporary glaciation will seem to roll back the hands of time. Even should the effects be far-reaching, mankind will again survive and regroup.

5 – ADAM: A HUMAN MENTAL BODY IN A HUMAN MENTAL REALM

The universal creation realm, as we discussed, is the dimension of creation and design of all things and the conceptualization of all objects in the physical universe, including man. It is the stage upon which the entire film takes place. On the universal mental plane, a decision was made to create, to bring about on earth an aware being, with his own mental body and his own mental realm. And the capacity to be aware that he is aware, and therefore the longing to reach total awareness.

A transformation had to take place. When evolving from to Homo sapiens, the new human being species was given both a mental body, and the option of building a human mental plane specific to man, which is called here-below life.

This mental body is a program, the soul of the human being; it has its own universal specificities consisting of data inherited upon its arrival, plus data which humanity has gathered through experience. It is therefore the sum of all the functionalities with which it was created, and a layer of beliefs

Talking about the human mental body is a prerequisite for understanding this plane. This plane does not exist fully formed in the vacuum of reality; it is derived directly from the universal mental dimension. It was not empty when the first human emerged, rather, it was already furnished with universal human laws. Think of it as a stage of absolute truth onto which is grafted the capital of what we as humans will accumulate during our time on Earth.

First, let's put some light on the human mental body that I like to call Adam (holy scripture figure), that we can also call soul.

The registered functionalities come with the source code, and are inherent to its nature. These inherent functionalities are in the first level. For instance, having a physical body, being born, living, breathing, eating, evacuating waste, and even the social custom of wearing clothes for protection, intimacy and beauty (this latter function is an example of something which took time to unfold, but it is nonetheless present in the source code).

Another component of this level is nomenclature, the naming of things. Any object or idea, when encountered for the first time, is named by the humans who discover or experience it, whether another being (perhaps newborn), a mathematical principle, the name of an existing street, or a planet. Identification by the senses leads to the creation of a name for the object.

Non-human life forms of the Earth recognize objects with their factory senses, (sight, smell, taste, touch, sound, and others vibratory translation tools which are sometimes much sharper than those of human beings), but they do not give these objects a name; naming something is a human specificity. This permits transmission of knowledge, allowing any new human arrival on Earth to save time in the recognition and application of practical things, and increasing the probability of its survival in this new space. And even without giving it any intelligent "human" explanation, we know for sure that man names everything he identifies and distinguish for the first time in his objective experience.

Man, like all living beings, also learns from instinct. The collection of data that comes to him through his senses, sounds, sights, fragrances, and others, animates and guides humans as to how to best react. Reflexes, survival, hunting (later making a living) for food and recognizing danger, all are inscribed.

There is also the notion of inheritance in the human mental world; not merely genetics, but the idea that knowledge, social codes, consciousness levels, and of course material possessions may be sourced from one's parents and community, carrying the torch of their ancestors.

Capitalism, which many seem to frown on these days, seems inherent in the human mental plane; it does not necessarily originate in recent centuries. Mankind has always tended to try to benefit from his experiences and achievements: the wheel begets the bicycle begets the motorized vehicle, each advance adding value. Every stone brings something new to the building. Aristotle and Plato led to Copernicus and Galileo, Newton inspired Einstein, and the list will go on.

The accumulation of knowledge leads to invention and discovery; knowledge gives us more clarity on our reality, and makes our stay on Earth easier. Gaining knowledge necessarily implies that we will develop standards (or laws) to manage it, resulting in more civilized behavior towards each other. The direct impact of inventions on laws and society is an undeniable fact. After the invention of the car, a traffic code became necessary once the use of cars became common. Capitalizing on the knowledge and discoveries of our ancestors means that we no longer need to draw water from a well to quench our thirst. Material and financial capital is undeniably a great resource written in the human mental body and realm.

Being able to apply acquired knowledge requires an intellect, an ability to recognize different facts, put them together, and reach a conclusion. This idea of reasoning will be discussed later in the chapter on mental faculties. Intellectual levels differ between individuals, so intellect is not automatic; it depends on each man's ability to reason outside of its mind, to comprehend and make decisions based on conclusions.

The direct consequence of this inherent mental capitalism is that people (through their mind) mimic other people. This happens all the time, but it is more instinctive for newborns and children.

This first level of the mental body – acquiring knowledge and learning to apply it on a personal level – tends to be developed early through education and the rules of society. On the other level, the capital of human knowledge acquired since humans first developed the capacity for complex thought is accessible. Herein lies a multitude of beliefs, ideas, desires, quests, questions, queries, aspirations, and dreams for humanity, collectivities, and individuals. It is a level that contains concepts about the universe, life, death, religion and science; both tales told from the past and visions anticipated for the future. They may be myths – tales which no man has actually witnessed – or they may be prophecies and predictions. This level helps us appreciate the extent and limit of our abilities, and leads to the conception and creation of new technologies, ideals, and concepts. And sometimes, in evolved individuals or societies, the idea of progress.

Some features of the mental body are optional: mating, childbearing, or choice of residence, for example. Some might say that working could be considered optional, but in truth, work is not an option; work is any activity that both aims at meeting one survival needs and also filling one's time on earth, whether the "work" is paid or unpaid. Once the basic needs for survival are met, one can work to expand levels of comfort and convenience, or reach a new level of achievement when he doesn't do the work to simply fit into a certain system.

In truth, the primary consequence of this mind specific to man is the desire, the will or the need to fill the time allotted on Earth with useful activity. Almost from birth and without even realizing it, humans seem to strive towards keeping active and growing.

This is the first level of the human mental body, but one's first experience with the mind is very different.

The mind is the conditioning, the paradigm, like a terrestrial program; a blank hard drive that a human is born with. Step by step, we pick up lessons from our environment like we download programs or upgrades – sometimes voluntary, sometimes automatically, often unconsciously, without the capacity to either accept or reject the information at first. The capacity to discern which lessons are valuable, which are trivial, which are not innate. This downloaded program, the center of my human nature, will rule my entire life but I do not know it yet. It is what enables me to locate myself in space and time, to acquire a new skill, to perceive the world as I integrate each element that I learn. Perhaps it is like a database, encompassing my entire cognition of the world; if new information not already in my program creates an "Error" message, I consider whether or not to supplement or correct the data. From the day of our birth to the day of our death, our perceptions and experiences shape the person we become; I am a direct consequence of my program. The human "me" is a direct consequence of my genes and conditioning.

When I mentioned in the previous passage that we might lack the capacity of discernment, I am referring to the fact that infants cannot yet evaluate information in a meaningful way.

Therefore, they do not have the means to accept or reject. They are subject to the ideas, beliefs, and behaviors which are taught or displayed. Whether presented directly or indirectly, such input is imprinted in the infant's mind. And as the human being has been designed to mimic from its first days by watching, learning, then replicating, this is how it is happening.

The result could be called personality, the subconscious mind, or the soul. Regardless of what it is called, it represents the individuation of each human. It is the central piece around which is built the detail of every human life on Earth, from birth to death.

The infant goes through many experiences as it grows, beginning with separation from the parent, going on to other complexes. The infant will experience betrayal, rejection, and injustice, as well as astonishment, joy, and discovery.

Everything an infant knows is what he has been taught; everything taught is called conditioning. From religion, to language, to morality (the notion of good and bad), the concept of money and value, the idea of a romantic relationship, the possibilities of work, friendship, life, death, all such concepts contribute to the building of the child's personality (and sometimes, many personalities).

The child absorbs these lessons to handle life better: to better integrate into a clan, or to learn self-defense. The child might then tend to the role of victim or offender, or alternate between the two. He might then develop kindness, or instead, bitterness. The resultant personality comes from a time when the child had no way of controlling how to interpret the events shaping him. All of society's standards, desires, and aspirations have been dumped on the child.

The mind is a paradigm made up of various beliefs, rooted in the association of events or people with conclusions assumed to be truths. It is one's scheme of thinking and logic, with no means to overcome the scheme, to think outside of its structures. Linear memory colors the concept of what is good and bad, and automatically censor results. This system of social development has been passed down from previous generations. The contents of this system change at a very slow pace, often to be replaced with a more comforting set of assumptions, judged in the changed system to be more appropriate.

One should not seek to destroy this mental that some call "ego." First, because it is impossible to destroy, and second because it can be a very valuable tool, and some of its contents can be very beneficial if acknowledged and well used. Rather, we simply need to verify its content from time to time. We should be willing to replace what no is longer aiding happiness or growth. To erase a belief, one must first become conscious of it.

In conclusion, think of the mental body as representing what is transmitted by the environment and accepted as reality. Activating an intentional, conscious mode, allowing us to better understand the reality by thinking it through, still awaits in a future version of ourselves. It is like an additional sense, a captor or controller of thoughts. This sense enables experimentation, identifying objects in a thought form, just as hearing leads to experiencing reality through a sound form. It also holds in memory, the most important and practical knowledge that one does not want to re-learn every new day.

The second layer to this human mental plane, is the *here-below* reality.

Here-below life, the life of man on earth, describes a space where man, who received a mental body, was allowed to create his own reality, which means being able to build a world that is superimposed on the universal mental plane.

When I say, "allowed to create," I do not really mean create from scratch. A better word would be transforming the space, the natural habitat, with its laws and functionalities into a system. It could be also a called a co-creation, where the first level, the raw material and the intelligent space is given, and upon which man sets a system.

Man uses wood to build a table, and he studies nature to put concepts into an understanding of reality.

That system that some call humanity world, here-below, or the matrix, is a man-made reality superimposed on the solid base Earth, and can in no circumstances be called life. Life is the mirror of universal creation, whereas here-below is the lifestyle man built on it, very often transforming from era to era, and more often becoming obsolete and re-built in continuous new ways.

Here-below, man's creation plan, consists in defining, inventing, designing paradigms like food, work, relationships, buildings, architecture, human laws, geo-politic, fashion, lifestyle, health, philosophy, communication, technology, education, money, exchange, growth, development, values and every concept or belief that pre-defines how life on earth for people should be or should not be.

The system, just like the mental body, does not come blank. It has imprinted codes like exchange, food, clothes, private property, building, mating, family, heritage, or justice, but those are not automatically activated. It is the evolution of societies and of humanity at large, through the crisis they go through, that provoke their activation and deactivation.

There are laws for society, the city, and every time a society goes through a crisis (economic, social, healthy, governmental) an opposition between forces that preach for the unique current of thought and others that fight for diversity instantly rises. Identity, segregation and superiority (in culture, race, religion, economics) parties may win for a little period of time, but the diversity, inclusive parties always end up taking back the equilibrium of life, as they are the most beneficiary for humans and life in general.

6.

THE SUBTLE BODIES, BEYOND PHYSICAL EXISTENCE

I have recognized my subtle bodies during my lifetime as a human physical being. And I think that everyone who has tried enough will find out their existence and maybe master their use. In general, people know that they have thoughts and that they have feelings. There is normally no need to argue about that.

But, what is causing some to be skeptical is the before birth and the after-death existence of their being, their transcendence and survival to physical experience. I, here in this chapter will merge mind and emotions in one body, the subtle body. Just like in the dream state, we usually experience them together through images, thoughts, feelings, etc. We might even call them soul (for the purpose of simplification), even though the soul is more a mind matter and feelings are prior to it. But as in general, the feelings are emotions that have been associated to beliefs, we can say that beyond physical experience this soul has very little power to change beliefs or emotions.

In fact, it might seem weird, but only in the physical plane can one, when all bodies existing together at the same time, change paradigms and command emotions. When physical plane disappears, it is normally not possible to do so unless helped. But that is going to take us out of the subject, we are here to talk about subtle bodies when not existing in a physical realm. I also want to share my view on the soul from a human physical point of view, and keep to myself any spiritual, philosophical or religious meaning or explanation as it would be very hard to make them experiential for the reader. Still, there is a lot to become aware of and to discover here. Knowledge definitely equals clarity and more freedom.

The invisible, subtle bodies exist before physical. For those who do not believe in any invisible world or Creator, remains the undeniable level to it, it is that normally a baby is first an idea in his parent's, family's, society's and even humanity's mind, as well as in the collective mind of his ancestors. It is eagerly waited for, or unwanted. It has been planned for, or happened as an "accident." It is also supposed to answer a certain desire and aspiration: having a baby of a certain image, growing up in a certain way, representing the family, the clan.

So, the idea of the baby starts generally before one's conception, when little, teenagers, young adults, or adults, the future parents think of having kids or not having them, in the future. It is also very thought about when the baby is in the mother's womb, parents are either excited or annoyed, waiting for the baby. Parents are in love or not, have planned for the coming or not, and so have their parents, the society, and all of humanity. A first child is different from the second or the third. The baby has already a role in their mind. It is called reproduction, but it is never indeed a real reproduction of his parents. A lot of factors are played in this game.

Some think we are overpopulating the planet, others think the opposite. Some are afraid of the expenses of having a baby, others believe they represent prosperity and hope. Some are longing to have a child desperately and will choose a mate randomly just to fulfill this need, while others have it all planned. Some receive years of treatments to have a child, others get pregnant every year. There is a scope on earth at each era, of how giving life, and bringing about humans is seen. A multitude of paradigms that have certainly evolved in a positive way, as we are far today from the idea of a kid being a slave to one's parent, or a kid having completely grown in the image of one's clan, or the idea that girls are a shame for the family, etc. Still, some insidious beliefs keep on displaying in a very symbolic way.

The idea of a baby, of bringing about life, already has its scheme globally, in the community and individually. Long time before its conception, and as it crystalizes as a fetus in a womb, the thought form becomes more and more solid. So, in a way, the soul of the baby is already here before its actual birth.

To go further, the baby's soul is a perfect replica of everything that is in the paradigm of his parents first, which most of the time, have this deep desire to break free from their mental heritage of their family tree or their society or human history in general. They do not know it consciously and tend to pass this heritage to their kids. We find this concept in the religious idea of salvation. One soul comes here for salvation from (unremembered) ancient sins. One does not understand! I have just been born, what sin have I committed? And yet, this beautiful (supposed to be pure) new soul is supposed to come here to gather paradigms and the break free from them. If you observe very little kids, you can see some who act like angels and others who seem to already have the hatred and bitterness of an adult who has been to war. It reflects a lot of things.

No real free will (which does not mean total free will) or real control of one's life is possible until the understanding of this. Parents, family, educational systems, society, science or beliefs are not to blame, they have been built in a way to serve a certain period of time until a higher perspective or truth comes along. And if all of these components do not agree with your will to do so, just do it in silence with the empathy that they have not come to the realization that their mind is generally not theirs, merely an inheritance, and some beliefs that they have accepted unconsciously.

Also, in the chapter on Adam, we can see that every mind has already been built in a certain way, has its source code. This means that one has already been designed in a certain way regardless of any paradigm and prior to any education or interaction with other humans. It is, therefore, undeniable that the soul, the mind, pre-exist physical existence.

For people who believe in the invisible, the soul is this personal vessel that has been given before physical appearance on earth that will go on forever and that one has to cleanse, protect, guide, and educate it in order to get the best ride possible.

On the other hand, after we die, we remain as a memory in our relatives and loved ones memory, or at least in the administrations records. Others remain for as long as humanity will go on. Think of Plato, prophets, Hitler, Newton, Pharaoh, Da Vinci. Their soul definitely survived their physical death. What is not so obvious is for the common people to realize this. If you have not been wildly known for your contribution to humanity or your destructive behavior towards it, does this mean that your mental body will die? Does it mean that you will not reach soul immortality? Of course not.

The notion of an afterlife (a purgatory) and "a hell and heaven" new physical reality, can be thought of as mirrors one of another. When we die, the majority of us automatically go to the astral world, we keep our subtle bodies, but we lose our physical one. In the astral world, we experience our beliefs of an after world just like in a dream, our ideas about after death, religious spiritual beliefs, implemented with the dominant emotion of our body. For example, one who does not fear death in a symptomatic way will visit light and nice places with mostly a nice dreamt life. The places here mean the scenery displayed. The scenery displayed will then depend on the paradigms about life and afterlife.

There in this afterlife, awaits the soul, for the universe to crush or to end, or to bounce back into a new one with new laws of physics or of another science that we will discover then, and will be displayed on the new earth and the heavens space, a new life for everyone to re-incarnate.

CHAPTER 3:

OTHER HUMAN FEATURES AND OPTIONS

1.

REASONING AND UNDERSTANDING HAPPEN OUTSIDE THE MIND

Suddenly one day, nothing made sense anymore. There were too many contradictions, too many opinions, and not enough evidence. The models I had applied to my world seemed to be falling apart. No landmark stood still, pillars erected on sand sank until they disappeared. Yet, there was more happiness than concern about the idea that the play would finally stop, that the truth, or even a small part of it, would emerge; it would be a simple process, but not an easy one. As I absorbed these revelations, I would tell myself, "Never mind, it won't matter."

Then the inevitable happened. What I had been running away from all my life caught up with me. Questions started to flow incessantly, day and night. No matter how much I tried to distract myself, nothing helped. Confusion set in.

Could I bear everything that was going to follow? Would I be able to question and investigate everything? Who was I to dare to ask such questions? What authority did I have? Questioning in such a manner has been prohibited. Only what the arbiters of law or faith have told me should count. I was not allowed to venture into this field where only the select had access, and even these select were prohibited from fields of other elites.

Those authorities of the world, holders of universal truths, had agreed on their boundaries; each camp was the product of a particular conditioning, a point of view specific to reality and existence, and no one could change sides during his life. Within each camp, it was they who had the capacity to understand everything, while all of the others had gone astray.

I realized quickly that such resistance was illusory, a mirage that I used to avoid taking responsibility for myself. It became clear to me that no one had ever forced me to do anything, let alone think. The truth was that I didn't want to grow, mature, and accept reason. Yet, at the end of my adolescence, I was now capable of using my discernment, checking the validity of my program, and amending it if necessary. To better understand reality, to distinguish the valid from the futile, there had to be a methodology and I had to discover it. It was something strange, as if I was a child again, full of questions, questioning all the answers I had been given, only this time I was questioning my own mind.

At birth, a child has no cognition of the nature of reality, let alone of the laws which govern it. No procedure manual or rule book is provided. As children grow, they detect and integrate information using the five physical senses, as well as emotion and thought. The observations thus accumulated would have populated an exceptional database from which we could have drawn conclusions about what reality represents, but a series of personal rather than universal explanations interfere with the interpretation of data so gathered. It seems not to matter, almost as if it was preferable to avoid understanding and to accept everything as taught, for fear of being separated again. Perhaps one of the aims of the game upon arriving on Earth is to correct some errors in understanding what reality is, taking humanity to a higher level of understanding of reality. I accept the challenge.

I am willing to turn back, to go the opposite way, to start from zero. I am told that it is a silly quest, that these are questions of children and I am an adult now. I respond, to myself, that what I am told doesn't matter; the possible discovery seems to be worth the exploration. I seek a more stable rock as a foundation, not suspecting that I will, in fact, uncover a cave of precious stones.

From the beginning of their journey on Earth, humans experience interest. As objects appear one by one on the screen of their experience, curiosity arises from the identification of a new object; the discovery intrigues them and attracts their attention. Not all objects have the same effect on everyone, but certain ones lead to the desire to understand more about them; hence the toy that a baby puts in its mouth. In time comes the realization that this object has a function, a mode of use, a story, and specific characteristics which the baby wants to understand.

One of the greatest thirsts for humans is to understand their reality. No cognition is satisfactorily accomplished without the moment of relief that results from an explanation, even a biased one. We have an innate need to establish a framework, to get our landmarks about a fact or an object so that we can move forward in life. The first attention to an object generates in us a silent thought, in a subtle and abstract manner: What are you?

This is the birth of our questioning about the reality as we experience it. We learn to eventually formulate our questions with words, asking out loud for answers from those we believe have all answers, the first adults we meet.

The personal, innate curiosity of the baby leads to the birth of questions about objects. Later, curiosity is generated by the various things and concepts which adults present, and will finally come in reaction to situations where the now-grown child does not understand a new situation and seeks explanations. The bottom line, then, is that prior to any treatment, processing, understanding, or apprehending of reality, we engage in questioning about the nature of things.

While this process is the intentional activity of dealing with an object newly experienced, it has nothing to do with the mind, and the need to question happens outside of it.

Consider again how the infant goes from non-awareness of objects as a baby to their recognition and relative cognition as a child. The process flows from the initial concreteness of everything, to the abstract rendition of specific things and concepts. I can see, feel, sense, hear, and even taste (with her milk) my mother, before understanding that this mother is a form that occupies space around me. I distinguish this form's existence in my field of experience; it becomes separate and distinct from the generic concept of "space."

Space, in my earliest awareness, is the container for all objects. Its contents – including matter, concept, thought, emotion, law, information, and sensation – represent anything that can be known. Physical space, emotional space, mental space, and etheric space are all separate dimensions wherein objects are found. As my exposure to the world of reality progresses, I experience other human forms, and I understand that there exists in this terrestrial experience an object known as a human being. I soon come to realize that even when a person no longer appears in my physical field of experience, they continue to exist. I then twig on to the fact that I, myself, am a human being; I'm learning to recognize my image in a mirror. At last, I am given a methodology to understand the questions I ask of myself, and how to search for consistent answers.

As previously discussed, a child at birth does not have the capacity for discernment or self-cognition; the baby needs a place to start the learning process. This place is initially the family, later will come school, and still later, society at large. The new being takes the torch of accumulated knowledge from his community, a place where his society has aggregated found knowledge and beliefs. If he then activates his mode of consciousness and realizes his true nature, he allows himself to re-evaluate the existing program. Organizing existing data, and perhaps acquiring new data, might result in better understanding, a better program, for his family, his society, and perhaps even humanity.

We should not consider this process as a fight against the existing, rather, it is a self-invitation to a more advanced form of thinking. In this space-time, the only freedom guaranteed universally and indefinitely is freedom of thought; violating this rule is the ultimate offense against humanity. It is morally wrong to manipulate, to insert any thought, to impose a particular idea upon someone as a mandate. It is the highest violation of the law of universal morality. Universal morality sets limits to our individual freedom to act, and allows the community, through its institutions, to intervene should a community member infringe upon another member in such a way. In society, everyone has a right to live in peace, everyone has the right to protection of their physical property. But nothing and no one ever has, and never will have, the right to control, manipulate, or limit the thoughts of another human being.

Children then begin to explore, first involuntarily, and then voluntarily, the concept of abstraction and the idea of the intangible. All the knowledge transmitted to me by other humans includes a description of the object, a statement of some of its specificities, and the object's name. Often, we taint a conclusion artificially established between me and the object, consisting of the perception that I will have about it now.

Any learning about anything goes through different stages: the distinction of the thing from other objects, and therefore its differentiation in space from those other objects. We are taught its identification, the code or the name given to the concept. We are taught its observation, sometimes a study by experimenting or theorizing it. We learn its evaluation, or relevance, and value whether we need it in our journey or whether it is something to avoid. Finally, we reach (or are taught) a conclusion about the object so that we understand it sufficiently to explain or describe it to others.

A standard reasoning is usually added to or included in this process; a logic often related to a correlation or cause and effect relation, which models my perspective on things, outside of which I cannot conceive. When I come to the realization that "I am not what I can observe," I distinguish several components of my being. By identifying these components, I can study them to finally understand that I am the master, and that they are there to serve the "I." These conclusions and observations allow me to have an overview, and to realize that the neutral processing of all information happens outside the mind on which is overlaid my program.

What is commonly called brain activity changes according to the achievement of this standard reasoning. In other words, my ability to reason, the logic by which a quest results in a discovery, largely depends on my awareness that I have a program, and that I can think outside of it. Questioning my paradigm never threatens my "I" (i.e. chapter on consciousness).

I discover that I am able to observe my thoughts, emotions, behaviors, and actions as perceptions of the world, and appreciate that this happens outside my body and mind and emotions. I think that the ability to partly take over this activity is triggered by the recognition of consciousness, of the nature of my "I." I am thus, above all, a human belonging to a community, mimicking (or rebelling against) all the habits and customs of that community. I am part of a collective system of validation or rejection, leading me to embrace the capacity for discernment, which leads to a better understanding of the world; a sine quinone perquisite for self-realization, and by definition, self-actualization.

Maturity of thought consists in not having a pre-established attitude of rejection or acceptance each time a new idea is offered to me. I should try to confirm the new idea's validity if I think it is relevant to my path of evolution. Greater mastery of this ability means ignoring the messenger and only focusing on the message. Effort is required to transform the person, speech, or situation, however repulsive, into a series of neutral information to verify.

While the process of discovery is often confused with the notion of "Spirit," the methodology is precisely the path that leads to more precise, valid truths. Reaching Spirit consists of each step that cognition takes to reach a higher relative truth from which the mind is detached; the hope is to be able to eventually access an absolute truth. Brain activity, as evidenced by thought, is the path by which I, the person, takes the path to the Spirit, should I so desire.

The end goal of the process is to reach understanding; a moment of "ah ha!" and relief, upon reaching the demystification of an object. It is like the experience one feels when a complex mathematical problem has been solved, or when one finally understands how to assemble a child's toy. Children want to connect with and explore the use of almost anything: toys, utensils, pillows, shoes, anything they encounter for the first time. They want to understand it, to know it in its essence. It is human nature to want to "know" because knowing allows us to attribute meaning, to incorporate predictability, to remove confusion. We wish to sweep away the mirages that we have allowed in our lives, to evolve towards a higher form of intelligence, to relativize our daily concerns, and transmute any excess energy towards the purpose of widening the scope of our experience. Knowing in a non-contradiction way. Because non-contradiction is the most important law of cognition.

Getting older broadens the scope of the "I." When I was 5 years old, I couldn't wait to be 30; there is no reason why, at 30, I would not love to be 83. Living a long life is not just getting older, it means going through each stage of humanity with the experiences it promises, in an evolving environment (architectural, cultural, social, economic, technological), in a body that is transformed throughout this journey.

Man comes to a great realization when he understands that there is no creation; nothing man "creates" truly comes from nothing. Rather, man transforms that which already exists. All objects exist before we experiment with the nature of their existence, as we try to better formulate reality as it exists outside of its acknowledgement by the mind. We experiment on objects, observing what happens to them as a result of our experiments. Brain activity shows us both the "Spirit" part and the "Illusion" part in this dimension of time and space.

The only reason why all this cognitive activity is happening is because our mind longs to reach completeness, meaning total knowledge and awareness. To become one with total awareness and knowing.

2.

ETHER IS INFORMATION ENERGY; SPIRIT VS ILLUSION

For the purposes of this book, the word "object" refers to everything that can be experienced in this space-time reality, given our current state of knowledge. This includes everything perceivable with our five senses supplemented by thoughts and emotions, whether tangible or not.

Living on Earth as a human means living in an objective reality; objective experience consists of everything that human beings can and do experience in the universe up to the present. An object is therefore any "thing" on which attention is focused, whether it is a relationship, a conversation, the taste of a brownie, the feeling of hunger, the thought of liking mathematics, the emotion of happiness, or the experience of riding a bike.

The world of the object therefore contains thoughts, emotions, sensations of the body, and perception of our surroundings. In the chapter on consciousness, we said that once consciousness focuses its attention on something other than itself, it is objective experience.

Between this formless (no objects, forms, concepts, colors, etc.) consciousness and our objective world (man and the universe) there is a bridge that allows the transformation from the state of being to the state of existing. That is to say, attention. Attention is paid to existing objects, meaning all forms of materialization of nature and man, all known concepts, regardless of their validity. And it is attention that discovers hidden parameters, notions, and materializations which have not yet been integrated or understood, or even imagined.

Ether belongs to the world of the object, and is an invisible dimension; an infinite and intangible space where all information gathered since the foundation of linear time and matter is stored. However, the ether avoids the notion of linear time (chronology, cycles, durations) and only knows the notion "here and now." In other words, it is present everywhere at the same time, all the time.

When it has accumulated sufficient mass, the energy of this potentially objective reality passes into the experientable world, containing all the information at the individual, collective and universal levels. Ether is the energetic world, a priori to the experientable world of matter; it is the vibrational equivalent of the world to which we have access.

This ether is divided into two facets, and is essentially a world of duality or polarity. These two poles of ether are *spirit* and *illusion.*

A distinction becomes necessary here, since many confuse ether with the spirit at large, or even worse, with intuition. Applying our capacity for discernment, it is essential to put our mind in order, even if it means redefining our concepts.

All that is experienced through the activity of the mind is what we know about experience. This knowledge of the mind comes from the available data around the person, and this data contains both spirit and illusion.

By *illusion*, I mean any information that is invalid, indemonstrable, unprovable, or unfounded; above all, permeable from the point of view of those who experience it. It does not resist the change of point of view. It is still known as a reality in the sense that it exists, but it is not true in the sense that it is not an element that can be applicable to all. Everything is real in this world, whether experienced individually, collectively, or globally, whether it is a question of feelings, thoughts, or perceptions. But while everything is real, not all reality is true or valid.

The reality of people in past times was that the Earth was flat, that it had an edge, and that the sun revolved around it. The reality of a particular older civilization was that certain phenomena of nature (fire, sun, or rain) were meant to punish people who had behaved badly. The reality of some societies was that some races are genetically and legitimately superior to others and that inferior races had to be eradicated. My personal, not too distant, reality was that birds could take me for a ride on their backs.

The reality, the experientable character of the illusion, shows us that it actually exists in our everyday life; if it does exist, it means that it must exist. The illusion has been imposed as a parameter of this game, this universal law, and it plays a role in the deployment of experiencing the universe in the consciousness of man.

Being real, it is therefore part of the polarity which generates movement and allows the passage or transition from the consciousness of Pure Being into the consciousness of Experience. It also enables the transition from an impalpable prophetic spiritual reality to true objective reality. The more the illusion grows and crystallizes in collective belief, the faster the process of accelerating the descent of the spirit, which will reveal the mirage, takes place.

In contrast to the idea of illusion which we have just discussed, the concept of *spirit* can be thought of as any information that is true, valid, and relevant, and which repeals and replaces everything that preceded it. It is The Supreme Law, a set of intangible and physical laws governing the universe as a whole (including the anatomical man), and governing morals in humans. It is also the meaning, the direction in which the world of matter, knowledge, understanding, and application of this law is deployed.

Think of the spirit as a stream of water. A stream follows its path, in which the illusion can throw a few grains of sand or stones, but the stream itself will never be stopped. Its flow can be accelerated, thanks to the action of man, and this acceleration could precipitate its outcome. This human action, too, is registered as law, permitted, but not imposed on the latter.

Just as the ether has two facets – spirit and illusion – the spirit can be compartmentalized into two dimensions: everything that relates to the entire universe (including the physical body), and all that relates to universal moral (or, the behavior of humans among themselves and with this universe).

Such a division is not absolute, nor does it include a reference to other forms that energy takes (such as a rock, or a heavenly body). This division concerns only man, because I, as a human, cannot experience anything but the human perspective. Perhaps when my body is absorbed into the Earth, some part of my being might be transformed into another form; then I could communicate my point of view as that form. At the moment, though, I am human.

The laws of the universe governing the world of matter can be thought of as equations; they allow the birth of the universe. They govern the different interactions that result in its evolution and expansion, and they determine its partial or final destinations.

The other dimension – the laws which govern the behavior of man – can be considered the universal moral or virtue.

Morality is composed of the set of human behaviors that society has agreed upon as integral duties, and therefore rights. They are applicable everywhere, at all times, in the interaction of man with man, and man with nature. It is universal; there is no distinction based on race or gender, class or religion, education or philosophy.

In essence, morality is the guarantor of the dignity, preservation, sustainability, and evolution of the human being. It can be a complicated matter, a concept that is subject to debate once someone asks who has the authority to define that which is permitted and that which is not. Who could enumerate the commandments of this law, which, by definition, supersedes all other laws?

The answer is simple: Man himself has such authority, provided he uses his innate reason and discernment in defining the behavior. It is not for us as individuals to ask the question of what we, as individuals, have the right to do to other individuals. Morality does not consist of applying a set of obligations and restrictions when interacting with another being. Rather, it is knowing how we ourselves want to be treated and applying it outwards. If I see something as a high injustice and supreme betrayal when done to me, I should put that on the list of things to avoid doing to others. Anything beyond morality which governs our behavior are merely customs, existing to serve a certain society in a certain period of time.

Ether is the information energy in a pattern that allows for the correct focus, timing, and mass to know when to apply that information in the world of experience.

3.

DESIRE: AN ENGINE FOR EXPANSION, A TIMELINE ACCELERATOR

As humans, we are cognizant of what we need to sustain our bodies. The needs of man in general are completely rational, and can only be evaluated in the physical world. This term "need" is applicable only in the world of matter; it refers to all necessary ingredients, which permit and encourage the continued existence in a functional anatomical body.

We need oxygen, we need water, we need sustenance in the form of edible, digestible food, and we need to eliminate waste produced by our bodies. We also need, albeit with less urgency, clothes and shelter which provide protection against the elements, predators, or other natural threats. Given the universality of these needs among humans, knowing that they have essentially not evolved in their essence through millennia and across cultures, I consider them as prerequisites for human existence and survival. They permit the platform upon which life and its expansion are built.

Anything beyond these needs, whether a thought, feeling, idea or concept, should then be called desires or wants. I *need* to eat, but I *want* tiramisu.

Confusing desires with needs leads man to go beyond, to

deny, or to despise his progress, his achievements, and his greatness. For instance, one could find it "normal" and "necessary" to have air conditioning in a vehicle, but the availability of an air conditioning option is the fruit of a desire to make a journey in the vehicle more comfortable. It's easy to forget that the cooling system in question was the result of years of passionate work by people who first simply wanted to reach and explore the possibilities of altering their environment. Only afterwards were the concepts thus discovered and applied to everyday practical life.

Having clarified this distinction between need and desire, the chapter can begin.

We seek to understand specific desires, to appreciate their function in any individual or collective expansion, and to know the conditions leading to the rise of each desire (its origin). Some people get bored when having no desire, others fear desire and try to switch this "button" off.

While hearing motivational speeches by those sharing their surplus of "positive energy" or enthusiasm is, in general, pleasant and positive, there is nothing more dangerous than creating such motivation in someone who is lost. Being motivated, pushed, and encouraged while in a state of confusion can be highly destructive. Keep in mind that before any movement is commenced, a direction must first be chosen; understanding and clarity must precede the spark of motivation.

We often take actions which are motivated by simply following the crowd, because in spite of all our claims of individuality, man is a social animal. We all want to walk together, either towards something or away from something. Therefore, we can easily be caught up in a flow of actions, initiatives, or causes that are not actually our own.

Consider that if I borrow an energy that is not mine and was not born inside me, if I give myself to a cause that has nothing to do with my own path, in the long run, I take the risk of losing my way. Losing sight of my own desires, my ability to expand beyond my survival needs in our common effort to "serve the All in our journey" is lost.

In exploring the reality of desire, I need do nothing but understand what I, myself, really want. When I understand that, I understand the expression of my consciousness, my "I," within the objective world. We must learn to separate what we *think* we want from what we truly want.

I understand that what I want can, by definition, only be what really matters to me. And what really matters to me is what the lack of harms me. Desire for a thing arises only from its objective absence, and therefore, from the feeling that results from the lack of it.

There is nothing pejorative in that statement. The fact that "I" desire something simply means that there is a void inside of me, a kind of missing piece that will help me complete the puzzle.

The abstract character of this impression of want, and the fact that it affects all of my signals, finds its physical equivalent in the outside world as an experience. The experience can result in the acquisition of a car, the discovery of a new country, or the learning of a new language; an experience that then becomes the object of my desire and my attention.

Let us then define desire as an inner call coming from one's consciousness (and *only* from one's consciousness) to grow and expand this same consciousness through the will to experience an external object.

Attention, will, and aspiration become merged, causing an effect of attraction spontaneously in an almost involuntary way, so loud that it cannot be ignored. It is as if all the options that "I" have to express something are combined to give a clear image of a pleasant feeling to come. The result is a chemical and organic reaction almost screaming at me: *"I" want this experience!*

Sometimes the desire is for a new reality, parallel to our daily life. At first, the newness of this sudden and unexplained "want" immerses the entire body in a panoply of sensations. It monopolizes our mind, making other thoughts fade away, blurring the quality of previous objects of our attention. The first effect of desire is that it takes us to this new vision of life in a blissful body enjoying the fruits of the desired experience. We think of the result of fulfilling our desire as a heavenly future that transcends all belief.

Initially, the desire may be so strong that it makes even the most aggressive and anchored beliefs subside into the background. Throughout the minutes, hours, and days which follow, the desire remains powerful. It is quickly caught up with by the mind, which gradually decreases its impact each time until it seems to be a ridiculous dream, an unattainable product of our imagination.

Most of the time, the mind makes us resume a "normal" life; the desire remains a spectator, waiting for us to focus on it again. The desire itself cannot do anything for us, except wait for the day when we will have the courage to put the mind in its proper place as executor and not director, to let the will of the "I" take back the power. For this "I," this consciousness, when it enters the world of experience, neither knows nor acknowledges any belief. It only admits the notion of integrity, derived from universal morality.

Perhaps the "true" desires, those arising from consciousness, have a very personal character; they could cause, when revealed to others, a certain relativization, or a lack of understanding of the value of the desired object. This is perfectly normal, of course, because desire is a personal thing which can only be understood by its holder.

Those who follow the deepest desire for expansion would also have a better chance of finding a possible mission on Earth, as explored in greater detail in the next chapter.

4.

THE SENSE OF A MISSION ON EARTH

Humans look for meaning; we seek to put the pieces of a bigger puzzle together, to understand. Long before the exploration of my inner being consciously began, there were subtle, almost imperceptible questions eating at me: What is all this for? How best should I spend this journey on Earth? Is there a purpose for my existence? What is life about? Why? And most importantly: *Am I doing things right?*

The problem with the "why" question is that it seeks an origin, a cause; that cause is itself a result, the effect of an earlier cause. This leads to never truly being satisfied with the answer, and in turn, one is made to believe there is no answer to the question. We must acknowledge that the way one asks a question is paramount, before we embark on any quest for knowledge. How we begin our inquiry can prevent the trap of more confusion and frustration.

This is how the idea of the possibility of an earthly mission stealthily crept into my mind. Could each human have a task to be accomplished in our allotted time? But long before this question arose, I had to solve the problem of my existence, and accept it completely. Once I accepted my existence, clues began to be revealed. That basic questioning about existence comes from a sense of separation; the individual human can believe that she is separate and apart from the universe.

Why does a fly exist? Because the universe needs its existence for whatever the extent of its life may be. I exist, and therefore I cannot not exist, since existence and nonexistence of the same entity cannot occur simultaneously. Since I exist, it means that I must exist. I accept.

I look around and see abundant beauty. The flowers are beautiful, and the stars embellish the sky. It seems undeniable that natural phenomena have an aesthetic purpose which inspires man. Following this logic, could it be that humans exist to look pretty in this painting? It is very possible.

The objects exist in a space which they fill. The universe is a space, and at the same time, it is the sum of stellar and terrestrial objects that compose it. Objects fill the universe, so perhaps I may be there to fill this space like everything else; there is no reason why I should be an exception.

Finally, each object in space has a function. For instance, from man's perspective, bees have a (primordial) function in life on Earth. This is valid for any object of this universe. So, why then, as an object in the universe, would I not have a function like everything else? The bee does not realize its function, yet from man's perspective it clearly has one. Knowing one's function does not seem to be an easy task for objects in the universe, but ignorance of its function does not mean the function does not exist.

Perhaps entities in a higher dimension observe us, study us, and write reports on our function in the universe, as beekeepers do in our dimension. Since I am not a being of a higher dimension, and therefore limited by my sensory tools and conditioning, I cannot know for sure, but I can still try to make some parallels.

Obviously, in the universe everything is at the service of everything else. Everything impacts the whole, moving together towards that which I do not yet know what, nor where, nor when. The notion of the function of humanity as a collective, as an object of the cosmos, is, like the rest of the objects, to serve the whole. Every object in the universe, whatever form it takes, serves energetically and materially. Just ask a physicist.

While we wait to receive (from the fifth dimension?) the report on the energetic and material function of man in the universe, science seeks its own answers. But I am interested in the individual function of man.

In truth, I want to know if I, as a separate individual, have a particular mission or task to accomplish; I want details. Beyond an aesthetic end, beyond the purpose of filling space, I have no doubt that I have a function as a human being.

The idea of a function as an individual should be explored. This possible individual function is more commonly called one's mission on Earth. Looking at my fellow humans, I see that there is a notion of profession or work; a kind of mission to accomplish, for which they receive compensation from other humans. Is this job our mission? Are hours of one's life providing service to others part of our purpose? This could be the beginning of an answer.

Without calling it a job (which has a more alienating connotation, and is somewhat tainted with effort and financial reward at the expense of inspiration) I would say that a mission is more. A mission consists of a series of successive tasks to be accomplished once revealed to the individual. Each task contributes in its own way to improving the living conditions encountered on Earth during our stay here. We march towards the best possible version of life between humans – a kind of utopia not necessarily to be achieved, but to be aspired to – and our total harmony and symbiosis with the cosmos. I am obligated to put my heart into it, and cooperate as much as possible with this vision. My job is to sow, but I may not personally enjoy the results; the harvest might be done by the next generation.

Is there a ceiling on the possibility of improvement of the human condition? On the possibility that we can improve our harmony with nature? We have no indication that there is. We could, theoretically, move towards a kind of earthly paradise where all desire manifests itself instantly; a place where the law of universal morality reigns everywhere, guaranteeing rights, protection, and above all, personal dignity, without the need for institutions to guarantee it.

An evolved society believes that such a world is possible, and seeks it not out of fear of reprisals, but because they understand that everyone benefits from such a world. Maintaining such a social state is the supreme interest of everyone. In such a world, every question leads to an answer, every problem has its solution. In such a world, questions and problems would not be seen as curses, but rather, as opportunities for the acquisition and deployment of greater knowledge.

Man would no longer live under the tyranny of discouraging thoughts and feelings. On the contrary, he could realize his full potential. Waste and shortages would not exist. Fruits fall from trees to spoil before being consumed and nature doesn't call it waste. The fear of death would be eradicated; the end of life would be welcomed because man would know that his stay here was temporary in the first place, and would have acted accordingly to fulfill his purpose so that the temporary life would be complete.

Think back to people preaching the meaning of a mission on Earth. I often found them too self-confident, too paralyzing, wanting to assign me a duty that I didn't want.

Some people understand that they are not there by chance. In a perfect continuum of the cause and effect which generates the natural phenomena that surround us, the laws that support this continuity suggest that chance has no place in it. There could well be a role that we fulfill without realizing it. How many times have I thought of an outcome as "chance" when in fact it was merely that the parameters leading to the event were still hidden or beyond my capacity to detect them?

The intuition that there is a unique role for each of us is fueled by the fact that no two people are alike. The individuality of the "I" crystallized in a person is undeniable. There is not one person on Earth with an exact replica. We vary by parentage, by birthdate, by physical appearance, by fingerprints. No two humans have the same experience, lived the same events and encountered the people in the same circumstance. This is a fact, a true reality which can never change, even from the seven billion perspectives of each of Earth's inhabitants.

The uniqueness of my person and of my identity means that, while the "I" of each of us is a common denominator – the consciousness of man, the *me* – the person who embodies this specific "I" is a unique and irreplaceable singularity.

My person, by channeling consciousness, is meant to accomplish a unique and individual task. So, perhaps I should take it as a game and not as a responsibility, trying to discover my individual potentials by following my inclinations, my centers of interest. I don't really know how it works, but the individual character of such a mission already predicts that the revelation of our individual mission is just as much a task to do alone.

5.

ATTENTION:
THE BRIDGE BETWEEN CONSCIOUSNESS
AND EXPERIENCING A WORLD

At birth, I was not conscious of my attention. In the beginning it was nothingness, pure consciousness, an awareness that is only aware of itself. There was "I" without form or color, without person or identity. Then perception becomes more vivid, and crystallizes in my linear memory. I am the consciousness which is conscious of itself, "I" am, period. Objects do not yet exist in my experience. Everything I "knew" belonged only to the reality in which I found myself, my experience of the moment – the world of time and space, of thought and matter.

Even the objects of a higher dimension, those which still belong to the ether and which are therefore neither experienced nor yet available to be experienced, are there waiting for my attention; waiting for me to apply my translation of their essence into concepts. I have constant and unlimited access to all these objects everywhere and at all times, thanks to all my senses – my five physical senses plus emotions body and thought. This access results in identification through attention.

I first smelled, tasted, felt, heard, saw, and integrated an image without realizing it. Then, my elders knowingly directed my attention towards something, as my knowledge of this something would be necessary for me to survive and grow in their environment. Finally, much later, I learned to use my attention voluntarily to focus on things which I knew would be of major importance or benefit to me. This latter way of experiencing attention is neither given nor automatic; it is earned by intention and practice. It starts with a survival instinct (to stay alive on Earth), and develops to fulfill a purpose of growth and expansion.

Attention is therefore a route, an access method, a unique bridge which exists between consciousness and cognition of a world. Attention is the bridge between baby and the world around him, and the result is a model of mind and body navigating in a universe with other bodies and minds.

Just as my eyes would have no value in total darkness, the "I" is only aware of itself; attention is the light which reveals any object in scope. It is like a lighthouse, helping to apply my senses to better understand the nature of my environment in order to navigate in this world.

In class, the teacher directs us to listen to her, since this part of the lesson is necessary to give context to the rest of the course. On the street, I hear construction nearby, and the cars on the street sound their horns. My emotional state tells me that I'm excited about playing in the recreation field later. A classmate sneeze behind me. I hear the wind blowing through the trees, as well as the song of the birds, indicating that their migration has begun. The teacher's perfume smells great, I am trying to guess its name. I note that her hair is beautifully styled, and think that she must have dyed it recently. My body informs me that it is starting to need nourishment; I am feeling hungry. I anticipate the weekend, and hope that my parents will take me to the cinema.

Each moment offers me an infinity of information delivered by my senses, capturing the state of certain objects inside and outside of me. I didn't consciously know anything about it; I didn't know anything about attention, let alone focus.

Attention, like the air that we breathe, is available all the time and is activated upon waking up. However, concentration or focus is only activated upon request. It can be activated voluntarily, usually due to having a great interest in the object being focused on. It can be invoked involuntarily, such as when hypnotized by a particular scene. Concentration can be forced under duress. Focus makes it possible to suspend the processing of unnecessary information which could interfere with the signal, without losing the available data.

While attention could appear to be free flowing, it is often restrained by our experiences and training to seem like a prisoner of the mind. Attention tends to be attracted to what is already in the mind, what the mind wants to confirm.

The development from consciousness to the experimentation of objects by my "I" is the most beautiful of the stories written for man. It encapsulates interest, astonishment, exploration, and self-discovery; the enhancement of the "I" and its wonderful mirror that is the universe at large. It is almost like a fairy tale, had it not been tainted by beliefs which filter objectively neutral information through our experiences. Perception is the end product of this process. The more the veils are lifted, the clearer the image becomes. The mind is necessarily tinged with hasty, unfounded, unprovable demonstrations which we must make efforts to overcome.

Humans frequently have a fear of questioning everything or possibly seeing a higher dimension. How often have the contemporaries of visionaries, revealing new elements of the cosmos, condemned said visionaries? Betraying your conditioning for a new truth is frightening. Losing your bearings, dropping a rope to catch another higher one, jumping between two rocks to go where the grass is greener, can fundamentally shake our confidence.

The term "attention" could almost be replaced by the concept of "awakening." It's the wake-up mode of the human being, the "I" (consciousness) paying attention to or being aware of a world. Attention itself happens by default, and is taken by the objects which come into our sphere of experience. We lose the capacity for attention only during deep sleep, or when we learn to redirect it towards consciousness; attention develops a conscious awareness of itself. An attempt to describe this total reconnection is found in the chapter on consciousness.

CHAPTER 4:

CONSCIOUSNESS

1.

WHO? WHAT? IS THE "I"?

When a physician asks if you are conscious, what she or he is actually asking is if you are aware of your immediate environment and what is happening around you. They are asking if your consciousness is in this reality, if you still belong to where we are.

Are you conscious of my voice? Do you experience hearing?

Are you conscious that I am asking you a question? Do you experience the understanding that the sounds I am emitting have meaning?

Are you conscious of the meaning of my question? Do you understand me?

Are you conscious that I need an answer to my question? The physician needs to know if you are still functioning, and are able to interact with us.

The verb "to be conscious" is generally related to the recognition of an objective experience. I am conscious that my body needs nourishment, or that someone is talking to me. Being conscious is always linked to the attention (e.g. chapter on attention) given to an object.

If I was not conscious of the amount of time an activity would take, it means that I didn't pay attention to the expected time required. In every objective experience, consciousness is attached to the attention given to a certain object or concept. I am conscious that you are talking to me. I am conscious that I did not behave well.

The question that arises is: *what is consciousness?*

Consciousness is, at the same time, the knower of reality (the experience I am aware of), the known reality (stage upon which experience is played and its objects), and the knowing of it.

It is also an obvious, innate certainty that I am conscious; that I am here, now, and when directed to objects, that I am on Earth in the experiential reality. Stage, observer, certain cognition that I am aware of what is happening around me now, and most importantly that I am aware that I am aware. For, only consciousness can be aware of itself, only "I" can know the "I" because being conscious is what enables me to recognize objects, therefor it is prior to any experience.

In the realms of objects, emotions, thoughts, body shapes, sensations, and perceptions vary from country to country, from home to home and even between people in the same household. The common point to every person's experience is that they are conscious of their being, of this happening. "I am conscious" is then equivalent to saying "I."

The only element with which I am born is "I," and it is the only element of my entire experience that never ceases to be, that never changes.

I am born, I am 5 years old, I am going to school, I play with my friends, I sleep, I eat, I am 25 years old, I am home, I am in New York, I am a student, I am working; experience never cease to shift, I, the experiencer is ever present, never changing. I like candies, I don't eat sugar anymore. I am fat, I am slim, I love rock and roll, I only enjoy the Rolling Stones, you are my shining star, my best friend moved to the other part of the planet, I love my grandma, my grandparents all passed away, and on and on.

My body changes, my beliefs evolve, my feelings vary even within the same day, and the people that I share elements of my life with come and go. Some have left my life, others have been erased from my linear memory. The only stable element that has never left my experience is the "I."

Unbelievable, no?

Why is it that, regardless of all the moments of joy and sadness and all these passions that I have felt over time, the evidence of my bodily changes as seen in photos of my 5 year old self, why is it that on this screen representing my lifetime on Earth, everything occurs and passes, everything transforms or changes form, but "I" always refers to the same "I"?

Simply because me, the "I," has nothing to do with what I have experienced, nor with my beliefs, whether chosen or imprinted. Me, the "I" is consciousness without experience, without any attention given to any particular thing, without name or body.

I then imagined that "I" born in another environment, a distant land, under another flag, reflecting a different culture, language, and belief system. My head started spinning, thinking of all those times when I told myself, "In another life I would have been X," or, "Oh, I admire this woman, of course she is the way she is, being born under different circumstances," or even, "If X did not happen, Y would not have occurred."

The truth was that all these affirmations came from me, the persona, an identity built upon a solid and specific linear memory, prisoner of an invisible, intangible cage. I realized that I have helped to build, or let build my own prison.

That day, all my landmarks shattered one by one, and other than the sun rising in the east, I was not left with many general truths. What is true must stay true; it cannot be assumed, or on the paradigm that I had decided could be trusted,

And there I was, as if restarting from the beginning, asking myself what could be bigger than anything I could think of or know about?

Who am I? Where am I? What am I supposed to do? Am I supposed to do something? Who is right? Who is wrong? What should I believe? Who can I believe? Most of all, is there truly a higher power, a creator to all that is? Or do I just believe in one because I was told it was true? A sudden thought came to mind: I was born with the "I" and it's the only thing that I have never abandoned and that has never abandoned me. It is the only element that I am certain to live and die with. It is the only valid experiential thing; all the rest is pure theory.

And so I began my exploration of the "I." Of my consciousness, of its nature and maybe functions, of its activities and the tools it had to express itself.

You see, the only valid question to me at that time was: Is life worth living, or not? Does it have meaning and purpose? Is it even relevant to ask if there is a meaning to all this? Was there an origin? Is there a destination? Is it a stage in a longer, perhaps infinite journey? Does randomness apply? And is the law of cause and effect unbreakable? Or, can I change the course of things while at the same time living within the framework of this game? What was my part to play? If I am an element of the whole, what part can I control and how?

After this tsunami of thoughts and events, I lay in my bed and pictured, one by one, all the people I considered "bad." I forgave them, and asked their forgiveness, because I was no longer in a position to judge anyone with certainty. I also pictured all the people I thought I had treated badly; I asked for their forgiveness, and I forgave them as well. It's as if the notions of victim and persecutor merge together in a larger concept: ignorance.

Then I felt something new to me, a concept that I had only known intellectually up until then: peace. I dared to wonder, if I can experience this feeling here, imagine what it would be there…

I slept that night, in my dreams visiting a garden where neither good nor evil exist, a place where only peace, love, and happiness existed.

I knew I was embarking on a new, challenging path, but I did not really mind. I wanted to find out more about myself and the world, and I wanted to visit that garden at least once more.

Possessing the only power that I required for this new path, self-honesty, I smiled at my reflection in the mirror and began my exploration of consciousness.

The persona is the identity, the necessary element for consciousness to know and to experience a world. Consciousness chose to reveal, blossom, appear by creating many realms and many entities. From the subtlest to the edge of incarnation. The world of creation and of experience is consciousness will, and deed. It does not mean to crystalize in the identity experiencer, or to lose any flexibility to return to consciousness to lose identity or to create another one.

2.

THE PLANE OF CONSCIOUSNESS

In the beginning, there was nothing. But here, "in the beginning, there was nothing…" makes no sense because there is neither beginning nor end in the plane of consciousness. Using words, concepts, threads, images, or even feelings would be dishonest. Or, maybe one would have to write all unconditional love and beauty poems, as love and beauty are the only elements that transcend the mind. And even there, there would be objects.

Indeed, how would one describe a plane where experiences and objects do not exist? To better understand it, I can equate this plane to the experience of deep sleep. Has anyone ever woken up and told a story based on their state of deep sleep, or been able to put words onto this state? Were they able to bring back memories, descriptions or information? No scientist, artist, shaman, or philosopher can speak of his experience in the deep sleep plane, simply because the experience does not exist and therefore no object has ever been encountered there.

This is why talking about this subject can be difficult, if not impossible. All that each of us knows with certainty is that there is a state of consciousness called deep sleep where thoughts, perceptions, feelings, and emotions do not exist. Our attention, the part of ourselves which perceives reality, has nothing to detect, and so dissolves into itself.

There's nothing to be aware of; there is only consciousness, and therefore only consciousness is aware of itself. Only "I" remains. "I" and nothing else, "I" aware of "I." This is the plane of consciousness. There is nothing concrete or abstract to bring back. We do not live in this state, but we visit it frequently in deep sleep.

Consider the three states of human consciousness: "I" am awake (I experience the world of objects); "I" dream (I experience all worlds except the physical); and "I" sleep soundly (I experience nothing). When I wake from sleep, I advance with certainty that I am conscious. When asked if I am aware, I answer almost instantly, "Yes." When asked how I know I am aware, most of the time I use my sensory factors as proof of my waking state in a physical body, in a physical world.

When I dream, I experience the mental world through sounds, images and my emotional body. I connect to memories in the form of images, sensations, and emotions. Or, I may connect to pure imagination through symbols, images of sensations and emotions.

When I sleep deeply, "I" am always "I," unaware of anything except for "I," and "I" return from it to visit dreams or a physical world. "I" never cease to exist when visiting this state, but my body, my identity, and everyone around me disappear. The "I" is the only component that keeps on being. In this deep sleep plane, I am no longer aware of my physical body and the rest of the universe, and my thoughts and emotions disappear. I no longer know my name, where I sleep, or next to whom I sleep. I no longer exist, I just am.

The etymology of the term "to exist" traces to the concepts "to come out of," "to manifest in," "to appear as an object in a space," or "to be momentarily, currently something." To exist is therefore any object which emerges from consciousness which momentarily takes a form. Is this not what I observe from elsewhere in the world and its archives? It is therefore during deep sleep that human beings automatically visit the plane of consciousness, and therefore "I" and consciousness merge to become one.

Consciousness contains everything, and is nothing. It is the state of being, but without existence. In this plane the consciousness is conscious of itself, but no attention is paid to any object. Attention is in standby mode, because there is nothing, no object, to focus on. Since being aware of an object is the basis of all experience, no object exists in my experience if I am not aware of it, if my attention through my senses does not detect it and therefore does not bring it to my attention.

The plane of consciousness is the plane of being and therefore the basis of all existence. Like a black hole, everything is sucked into it, and comes out of it. This is the "restart" button, a place without form, size, age, duration, or cycle. Here can exist the promise of eternal peace, of perpetual happiness, of always possible renewal. Consciousness has no source, but is the source of everything. It is the origin of the origin.

This plane is therefore a space of peace, of silence of the mind, of absence of any terrestrial distraction or any other dimension or plane. Here is the pure state of all "things" – the human being understood, its true nature, that from which body, mind, and all notion of being emerge. Man, and the universe to which he belongs, finds its source and its backdrop in this pure consciousness, where everything merges to be one, to be nothing, to do nothing.

"I" has no origin, but is the origin of everything. It has neither beginning nor end, but everything begins in it to find its end.

From a human point of view, the beginning of the universe and one's own birth on Earth are the same. Similarly, the end of the universe and one's death are the same. Indeed, what difference is there between the day of my death and disappearance from this physical terrestrial plane, and the end of the universe (Armageddon)? The two events definitively stop my experience of a body and a mind in this plane, which is life here below on Earth, and so does deep sleep, the only difference being that I reappear in the same plane when I wake up.

I do not know why the consciousness, the "I," decided to generate an awareness of something other than itself, a world where certain entities (in this case, humans) are aware of things other than themselves – a world of experience, identification, differentiation and awareness of each of these. In any case, this plane, this being, had this irreversible intention, this irrevocable decision; and from there was born the universal mental plane, a realm of legislation of the creation of all things where order prevails. Such universal laws, if something other than the plane of consciousness had created them, would have defaults, would know coincidences and chance. And, maybe from my human perspective, I long to be one with consciousness, perhaps before I die.

The consciousness was then succeeded by the intention of this creation. It started with a mental activity, a dream, which then materialized in the physical world, more commonly called the universe that we know today, and that our scientists are trying to describe. Now we can begin enumerating the other planes, since after the foundation we have laid in this and previous chapters, the world of experience begins, objects take shape, and therefore speech is allowed.

3.

THERE AND BACK TO CONSCIOUSNESS: PEACE OF MIND

Peace of mind means a calm, at ease, and reassured mind. A pure place of being, a connection to the pure self, reached through meditation, prayer, or in a pure knowing and absence of worried doubts state.

The human who experiences life on Earth often confuses his non-objective nature, consciousness (the "I"), with the succession of moments when attention is focused on an object: work, health, entertainment, the household, imagination, desire, to name but a few. When becoming one with the experience, a person crystallizes into an identity.

In deep sleep, the attention of the "I" falls back into itself; "I" is only aware of itself. There is only consciousness. The "I" is in a space without objects, where "all" is absent. In this space, the vital functions of my anatomical body continue to function normally: my heart beats, I continue to breathe, everything is taken care of. Only my attention is on standby.

My body continues to exist, the planet continues to spin, trees grow, and people are busy all over the globe. When I wake up, my attention is activated again. The journey of a human being – this journey being known as life in general – happens through successive moments when attention is focused on experience, the tasks to be accomplished, and others when attention is on an forced off-mode (deep sleep). Very few people go to this state of non-experience intentionally.

I began being taught everything about what was known about the world as soon as I came out from my mom's belly, as humans used my attention to make me experience the worlds of mind and matter. I was never told anything about the nature of the "I" or whether it was possible to relive the moment when "I" was simply itself, with no object.

Perhaps it is not the role of others to explain it to me; perhaps it is impossible to conceptualize consciousness *to* itself until it becomes conscious *of* itself. Maybe the experiment had to reach its climax, each at his own pace, to lift the veil of illusion that there is something beyond consciousness experiencing a world of matter through the interface of the mind. Some rules of this matrix are still beyond our understanding.

The emotions play a primordial and undeniable role in this return to square one. For when one comes to visit emotions that relax the body more often and downplay the tyranny of the mind, something chemical seems to inexplicably allow the creation of an internal environment conducive to the emergence of reason and discernment. These are conditions imperative for the emergence of the recognition of consciousness as such.

To recognize and revive the consciousness, to live in the "I" when the man is awake, is more commonly called "inner peace" or "peace of mind." Many people who lived in earlier times confused peace with an emotion or a state of mind, but peace is the absence of emotion, sensation, thought, or perception. It is the nature of the "I," its state outside the world of the object.

Anyone with a goal walks towards it, hoping to achieve inner peace once the object of his or her attention has been reached.

For example:

Person A: What do you want?

Person B: I want the latest car.

Person A: Why?

Person B: Because that is what I want now!

Person A: What is it going to bring you?

Person B: Well, I'll feel good in the holding of it. It will make me happy.

Person A: Oh, so what?

Person B: And then I will be at peace.

This is, of course, merely an example. I leave you free to replace looking for a car with seeking an ideal companion, striving for a dream body, yearning for millions in the bank, acquiring a substance to consume, getting your degree, or any other promising object according to the unique interests and preferences of each one of you. Eventually, the goal is reached (or not), but peace itself is often postponed. Some would even think of peace as not part of this world.

Does this mean that any pursuit of a dream or desire is futile in the search for peace? Absolutely not. It is just necessary to recognize that inner-peace is a state which you do not need to deserve or chase, and which is available here at all times to you. A place, a garden, where the human being immerses himself in his essence, in a consciousness that experiences nothing but itself. On the other hand, a desire, when inspired by a conscious mind at peace, leads to an expansion: of the person, of the identity, and sometimes even of the entire community. But this expansion in no way impacts the "I" outside of matter, time, or physical space. The nature of "I" is peace, its normal state. There is no quest outside the self, nor a more conducive path to this meeting. The only thing to do is to recognize it and succumb to it.

This peace echoes in you every day, all day long. It calls to you with a soothing, loving, comforting voice. Come back to me, I am here everywhere, every time with, here with you. Come back to me and recharge. Come back to me and understand. Come back to me and feel it, feel your nature, feel your worthiness, the entire universe is here for you.

About the Author

Mouna Saquaque has always lived with the echo of existential questions: Who am I? Why am I here? Where am I? Where do I come from? What am I supposed to do? Am I doing things right? Where am I going? Is there a purpose to existence?

When she finally embarked in answering these questions, she started sharing her understandings by translating them to writings and meditations on life, from a *human perspective*.

She used to believe, and now knows, that the most important experiences to instill in one's life are *happiness* and *peace of mind*.

Finding the balance between making things happen and letting things happen. A game of cooperation between life unfolding and human expressions of existence, where self-knowledge is key.

You may also visit the author's website
for more interaction at:

www.MounaSaquaque.com

With every donation, a voice will be given to the creativity that lies within the hearts of our children living with diverse challenges.

By making this difference, children that may not have been given the opportunity to have their Heart Heard will have the freedom to create beautiful works of art and musical creations.

Donate by visiting

HeartstobeHeard.com

We thank you.